SHAH MOHAMMED

The Timeless Laws of Branding

The Hidden Keys to Crafting Iconic Brands

Copyright © 2024 by Shah Mohammed

All rights reserved. No part of this publication may be reproduced, stored or transmitted in any form or by any means, electronic, mechanical, photocopying, recording, scanning, or otherwise without written permission from the publisher. It is illegal to copy this book, post it to a website, or distribute it by any other means without permission.

First edition

This book was professionally typeset on Reedsy.
Find out more at reedsy.com

Contents

I Part 01—Brand Foundation

1 The Law of Customer-Centricity   3

II Part 02—Defining Your Brand's Strategic Foundation

2 The Law of Value Proposition   11
3 The Law of Niche   17
4 The Law of Focus   23
5 The Law of Positioning   27
6 The Law of Differentiation   32
7 The Law of Purpose   37
8 The Law of Authenticity   41

III Part 03—Brand Identity

9   The Law of Simplicity   47
10 The Law of Personality   52
11 The Law of Voice & Tone   59
12 The Law of Storytelling   65
13 The Law of Visual Design   71
14 The Law of Consistency   77
15 The Law of Archetypes   81
16 The Law of Timing   86

IV Part 04—Brand Experience

17	The Law of Experiential Branding	95
18	The Law of Holistic Experience Design	99
19	The Law of Overdelivering	105
20	The Law of Consistency (Experience)	109
21	The Law of Interactivity	114
22	The Law of Personalization	119
23	The Law of Emotional Connection	124
24	The Law of Building Relationships (With Customers)	128
25	The Law of Community	132

V Part 05—Brand Communication

26	The Law of Clarity	139
27	The Law of Emotional Appeal	143
28	The Law of Thought Leadership	147
29	The Law of Public Relations	152
30	The Law of Social Media	155
31	The Law of Listening	158
32	The Law of Authenticity(Communication)	161

VI Part 06—Brand Evolution

33	The Law of Extension	167
34	The Law of Evolution	172
35	The Law of Agility	180
36	The Law of Innovation	184
37	The Law of Resilience	188

Conclusion	192
About the Author	196
Also by Shah Mohammed	198

I

Part 01—Brand Foundation

1

The Law of Customer-Centricity

In the world of branding, there is one fundamental law that stands above all others: The law of customer convenience. This law states that the customer should be at the heart of every branding decision and action. It is the foundation upon which all other branding laws are built.

At its core, branding is about creating a promise and an emotional connection with your target audience. To achieve this, you must deeply understand your customers – their needs, desires, pain points, and expectations. Only by putting yourself in your customers' shoes can you create a brand that truly resonates with them.

The Law of Customer-Centricity requires a shift in mindset from **"What can we sell?"** to **"What do our customers need, and how can we best serve them?"** This customer-centric approach guides every aspect of your brand, from your brand strategy and identity to your communication, experience, and evolution.

To apply the Law of Customer-Centricity, start by conducting thorough research to gain insights into your target audience. Use a combination of quantitative methods (such as surveys and analytics) and qualitative methods (such as interviews, observational research, and focus groups) to gather data and uncover meaningful insights.

Next, use these insights to inform your brand strategy. Define your brand's unique **value proposition and positioning** based on what matters most to your customers. Craft a brand promise that addresses their needs and desires, and ensure that every touchpoint of your brand consistently delivers on that promise.

As you develop your brand identity, keep your customers at the forefront. Choose visual elements, a tone of voice, and messaging that will resonate with them on an emotional level. Tell authentic stories that showcase how your brand understands and serves their needs.

When communicating with your customers, prioritize clarity, empathy, and engagement. Listen actively to their feedback and adapt your brand based on their evolving needs. Build relationships and foster a sense of community around your brand.

Across every brand experience, strive to exceed customer expectations. Deliver consistent quality and value, and look for opportunities to surprise and delight. Continuously measure and monitor customer satisfaction and loyalty, and use these insights to guide your brand's evolution.

Remember, the Law of Customer-Centricity is not a one-time exercise but an ongoing commitment. As your customers' needs and preferences change over time, your brand must adapt accordingly. By keeping the customer at the heart of your branding efforts, you'll build lasting relationships, foster loyalty, and create a strong, enduring brand.

In the following chapters, we'll explore the other laws of branding, all of which build upon this foundational Law of Customer-Centricity. By understanding and applying these laws, you'll be well on your way to building a brand that not only resonates with your target audience but also drives long-term success for your business.

Airbnb: Building a Brand on Unmet Customer Needs

In 2007, Brian Chesky and Joe Gebbia, the founders of Airbnb, were struggling to pay their rent in San Francisco. They noticed that all the hotels in the city were booked up due to a big design conference, and many attendees were struggling to find affordable accommodations.

Chesky and Gebbia saw an opportunity to meet this unmet need. They bought a few air mattresses and offered their apartment as a cheap place to stay for conference attendees. They called their service "Air Bed and Breakfast."

This initial idea quickly grew into a larger vision. Chesky and Gebbia realized that there were many people around the world who were looking for unique, affordable, and local travel experiences. Traditional hotels were often expensive and impersonal, and they didn't give travelers a sense of connection to the places they were visiting.

Airbnb's brand was built around the idea of belonging anywhere. The company's mission was to create a world where anyone could feel at home, no matter where they were. This brand promise resonated with travelers who were looking for authentic, local experiences.

As Airbnb grew, it continued to put the customer at the center of its branding efforts. The company invested heavily in creating a trusted, secure platform where hosts and guests could connect with confidence. It created a review system that helped build trust and transparency, and it offered 24/7 customer support to address any issues that arose.

Airbnb also used storytelling to showcase the unique experiences its customers were having around the world. Its "Belong Anywhere" campaign featured real stories of hosts and guests connecting across cultures and forming meaningful relationships. These stories helped create an emotional connection with the brand and reinforced its promise of belonging.

By identifying and addressing an unmet customer need, Airbnb was able to build a strong, differentiated brand that has disrupted the traditional hospitality industry. Today, Airbnb is valued at over $100 billion and has served over 1 billion guests worldwide.

Warby Parker: Disrupting the Eyewear Industry with Customer-Centricity

In 2010, four friends - Neil Blumenthal, Andrew Hunt, David Gilboa, and Jeffrey Raider - were discussing how expensive and inconvenient it was to buy prescription glasses. They had all experienced the frustration of paying hundreds of dollars for a single pair of glasses, and they knew that many people couldn't afford this expense.

The four friends saw an opportunity to meet this unmet need. They realized that by designing their own glasses and selling them directly to consumers online, they could offer high-quality, stylish eyewear at a fraction of the price of traditional retailers.

Warby Parker's brand was built around the idea of making eyewear accessible and affordable for everyone. The company's mission was to provide customers with an easy, enjoyable, and socially conscious way to buy glasses.

From the beginning, Warby Parker put the customer at the center of its branding efforts. The company offered a home try-on program that allowed customers to select five pairs of glasses to try on at home for free, with no obligation to buy. This program addressed the common customer concern of not being able to try on glasses before buying them online.

Warby Parker also invested heavily in customer service, with a team of friendly and knowledgeable advisors available to help customers find the perfect pair of glasses. The company offered free shipping and returns, and it had a generous 30-day return policy.

In addition to its focus on affordability and convenience, Warby Parker also built its brand around the idea of social responsibility. For every pair of glasses sold, the company donates a pair to someone in need through its "Buy a Pair, Give a Pair" program. This program helped create an emotional connection with customers who valued socially conscious brands.

By identifying and addressing the unmet needs of customers in the eyewear industry, Warby Parker was able to build a strong, disruptive brand that has transformed the way people buy glasses. Today, Warby Parker is valued at over $3 billion and has sold millions of pairs of glasses worldwide.

This example demonstrates how the Law of Customer-Centricity can guide every aspect of brand building, from the initial product design to the ongoing customer experience and social impact. By deeply understanding and serving your customers' needs and desires, you can create a brand that stands out in a crowded market and drives long-term success for your business.

In conclusion, the Law of Customer-Centricity is the foundation upon which all successful brands are built. By identifying and addressing unmet customer needs, brands like Airbnb and Warby Parker have been able to create strong, differentiated identities that resonate with their target audiences. Putting the customer at the heart of every branding decision and action is not just a strategy – it's a mindset that guides every aspect of brand building, from product design to marketing to customer service. As you develop your own brand, remember that understanding and serving your customers' needs and desires is the key to creating a brand that stands the test of time.

* * *

II

Part 02—Defining Your Brand's Strategic Foundation

2

The Law of Value Proposition

At the heart of every successful brand lies a compelling value proposition. The Law of Value Proposition states that a brand must clearly communicate the unique value it offers to its target audience. This value should be distinct from competitors and directly address the needs, desires, and pain points of the brand's ideal customers.

What is a Value Proposition? A value proposition is a clear, concise statement that explains how a brand's products or services benefit its customers. It communicates the tangible results a customer can expect from choosing the brand over its competitors. A strong value proposition should answer the question, "Why should I choose your brand?"

The key components of a value proposition include:

1. The target customer: Who is the brand's ideal customer?
2. The problem or need: What problem does the customer face, or what need do they have?
3. The solution: How does the brand's product or service solve the customer's problem or meet their need?
4. The benefits: What specific benefits does the customer gain from choosing the brand?
5. The differentiator: How is the brand's solution unique or better than competitors'?

Why is a Strong Value Proposition Important? In today's crowded marketplace, customers are bombarded with countless brands vying for their attention. A strong value proposition cuts through the noise and clearly communicates why a brand is the best choice for its target audience. It helps customers quickly understand what the brand offers and how it can benefit them.

A compelling value proposition can help a brand:

1. Attract and retain customers
2. Differentiate itself from competitors
3. Guide product development and marketing efforts
4. Create a strong, cohesive brand identity

Examples of Strong Value Propositions

1. **Slack:** "Slack is the collaboration hub that brings the right people, information, and tools together to get work done."
2. **Uber:** "Tap the app, get a ride. Uber is the smartest way to get around."
3. **Dollar Shave Club:** "A great shave for a few bucks a month. No commitment. No fees. No BS."

In each of these examples, the brand clearly communicates its target customer, the problem it solves, the solution it offers, the benefits the customer can expect, and how it differs from competitors.

Crafting Your Brand's Value Proposition: To develop a strong value proposition for your brand, start by deeply understanding your target audience. Conduct market and user research to identify their needs, desires, and pain points. Then, analyze your brand's unique strengths and differentiators.
Ask yourself:

1. What does our brand do better than anyone else?

2. What unique benefits do we offer our customers?
3. How do we solve our customers' problems or meet their needs in a way that competitors don't?

Use the answers to these questions to craft a clear, concise value proposition that communicates the core value your brand offers to its target audience.

Remember, your value proposition should be more than just a slogan or tagline. It should guide every aspect of your brand's strategy, from product development to marketing to customer service. By consistently delivering on your value proposition, you'll build trust, loyalty, and long-term success for your brand.

Dollar Shave Club

In 2011, Michael Dubin, the founder of Dollar Shave Club, noticed that many men were frustrated with the high cost and inconvenience of buying razor blades. Traditional razor brands like Gillette and Schick charged high prices for their blades, and men often had to go to the store each time they needed to replace their blades.

Dubin saw an opportunity to solve this customer problem. He conducted market research and found that many men were interested in a more affordable, convenient way to buy razor blades. Based on these insights, Dubin developed a simple yet compelling value proposition for Dollar Shave Club: "A great shave for a few bucks a month. No commitment. No fees. No BS."

This value proposition addressed the key pain points and desires of Dollar Shave Club's target audience:

1. **Affordability:** "A great shave for a few bucks a month" communicates that customers can get a quality shave at a lower price than traditional brands.
2. **Convenience:** By offering a subscription service that delivers blades

directly to customers' doors, Dollar Shave Club eliminates the need for men to go to the store to buy blades.
3. **Flexibility:** "No commitment. No fees." emphasizes that customers can cancel their subscription at any time without penalty, giving them greater control and flexibility.
4. **Transparency:** "No BS" suggests that Dollar Shave Club is a straightforward, honest brand that doesn't rely on gimmicks or hidden costs.

Dollar Shave Club's value proposition became the foundation of its brand identity and marketing efforts. The company's launch video, which went viral in 2012, showcased Dubin himself explaining the value proposition in a humorous, relatable way. This video helped establish Dollar Shave Club as a fresh, disruptive brand that understood its customers' needs and desires.

As Dollar Shave Club grew, it continued to evolve its product offerings and marketing strategies, but always stayed true to its core value proposition. By consistently delivering on its promise of affordable, convenient, flexible, and transparent razor subscriptions, Dollar Shave Club built a loyal customer base and established itself as a major player in the men's grooming industry.

In 2016, just five years after its launch, Dollar Shave Club was acquired by Unilever for $1 billion, a testament to the power of a strong, customer-centric value proposition.

Amazon

In the mid-1990s, Jeff Bezos recognized the potential of the growing internet and saw an opportunity to revolutionize the way people shop for books. At the time, brick-and-mortar bookstores were limited by physical space and typically carried only a small fraction of the books in print. Bezos believed that an online bookstore could offer customers a much wider selection and a more convenient shopping experience.

Bezos and his team conducted extensive research on customer preferences and pain points in the book-buying process. They found that customers often struggled to find the books they wanted in local bookstores and were frustrated by the lack of selection. Customers also valued competitive prices and the ability to easily browse and discover new books.

Based on these insights, Bezos developed Amazon's initial value proposition: "Earth's Biggest Bookstore." This value proposition communicated several key benefits to customers:

1. **Wide Selection:** "Earth's Biggest Bookstore" suggests that Amazon offers an unparalleled selection of books, far beyond what any physical bookstore could offer.
2. **Convenience:** By shopping online, customers could easily find and purchase the books they wanted without having to visit multiple physical bookstores.
3. **Competitive Prices:** Amazon committed to offering low prices on its books, making it an attractive alternative to traditional bookstores.
4. **Discoverability:** Amazon's website was designed to help customers easily browse and discover new books through features like book recommendations and customer reviews.

Amazon's value proposition resonated strongly with book lovers and quickly set the company apart from traditional bookstores. As Amazon grew, it continued to expand its product offerings and improve its customer experience, but always stayed true to its core value of putting the customer first.

Over time, Amazon's value proposition evolved to "Earth's Biggest Selection," reflecting its expansion into new product categories beyond books. However, the company's focus on wide selection, convenience, competitive prices, and discoverability remained constant.

By consistently delivering on its customer-centric value proposition, Amazon has become one of the world's most valuable and influential companies, revolutionizing not only e-commerce but also industries like cloud computing, streaming, and logistics.

In conclusion, the Law of Value Proposition is a critical foundation for any successful brand. By deeply understanding your target audience's needs, desires, and pain points, you can craft a compelling value proposition that communicates the unique benefits your brand offers. This value proposition should guide every aspect of your brand's strategy, from product development to marketing to customer service. As the examples of Dollar Shave Club and Amazon demonstrate, a strong, customer-centric value proposition can be the key to disrupting industries, building loyal customer bases, and achieving long-term success. As you build your own brand, make sure to invest time and effort into developing a clear, differentiated value proposition that resonates with your ideal customers.

* * *

3

The Law of Niche

Most of us dream of building a company that would be called the next Amazon or Apple. However, we have to realize that Amazon and Apple started small before becoming influential in their respective fields. In the early stages of brand development, it's essential to focus on serving a specific niche market. The Law of Niche states that brands should initially concentrate their resources on meeting the unique needs of a well-defined target audience rather than attempting to appeal to a broad market. By focusing on a niche, brands can differentiate themselves, establish expertise, and build a loyal customer base that will serve as a foundation for future growth and expansion.

Several successful brands have followed this approach. Macintosh began its business by targeting a niche customer base of graphic artists and designers in Fortune 500 companies. These designers used Macintoshes to give presentations to marketing professionals and executives, who were mesmerized by the GUI and responsiveness of the computer. They began to use Macintoshes for their own work and gave presentations to outside vendors, publishers, and clients, spreading the idea and helping Macintosh dominate the market.

Similarly, Documentum introduced the Electronic Document Management System (EDMS) in 1993 by targeting the regulatory affairs department in Fortune 500 pharmaceutical companies, where the user pain was high due to the need to file a minimum of 250,000 to 500,000 documents. The system then penetrated other departments within these companies, such as research, manufacturing, plant construction and maintenance, and eventually expanded to external vendors, contractors, and other industries like regulated chemicals, oil refineries, and exploration and production. EDMS continued to grow its market, reaching IT departments, real estate divisions, Wall Street, and finally, the swaps and derivatives business.

Another example is Walmart, which Sam Walton initially started in small towns with populations not exceeding 5,000. By focusing on these niche markets, Walmart was able to establish a strong foothold and gradually expand to become the retail giant it is today.

The rule of thumb for business success is to start small, find the target market with maximum pain, focus on a particular need, work on it, make your product distinctive, and dominate the niche market. Once you become a leader in the niche market, you can move to larger markets. Focusing on a smaller customer segment makes it easier for the entire company to concentrate its resources, energy, and efforts on meeting the specific needs, wants, and desires of that niche. This focus helps in developing and launching a meaningful product at a lower cost, and a better product means loyal customers.

Targeting a niche market also facilitates testing and collecting efficient customer feedback about the product or service, which aids in further enhancing the offering. A niche market helps a business perfect its process through innovation.

The Benefits of Targeting a Niche Market

1. **Differentiation:** By focusing on a specific niche, brands can develop unique products, services, and messaging that set them apart from competitors. This differentiation helps brands establish a clear identity and attract customers who are seeking specialized solutions.
2. **Expertise:** When brands concentrate on a niche, they can develop deep expertise in their target audience's needs, preferences, and pain

points. This expertise allows brands to create more relevant and valuable offerings, leading to higher customer satisfaction and loyalty.
3. **Resource Efficiency:** Targeting a niche market allows brands to allocate their resources more effectively. Instead of spreading resources thin across multiple customer segments, brands can focus on delivering exceptional value to their core target audience. This focus leads to better returns on investment in product development, marketing, and customer service.
4. **Loyal Customer Base:** Niche audiences often have strong, unmet needs. By catering to these needs, brands can foster a sense of loyalty and advocacy among their customers. These loyal customers can become powerful brand ambassadors, helping to drive word-of-mouth marketing and organic growth.
5. **Reduced Competition:** Niche markets often have less competition compared to broad markets. By targeting a specific niche, brands can avoid direct competition with larger, more established players and carve out a profitable market position.

Examples of Successful Niche Targeting

1. **Bonobos:** Bonobos initially focused on solving a specific problem for a niche audience: providing well-fitting, stylish pants for men who struggled to find off-the-rack options that fit properly. By concentrating on this niche, Bonobos developed expertise in men's fit and style preferences, leading to a loyal customer base and eventual expansion into other product categories.
2. **Starbucks:** When Starbucks first opened in Seattle in 1971, it focused on a niche market of coffee connoisseurs who appreciated high-quality, freshly roasted coffee beans. By targeting this niche and educating customers about the art of coffee-making, Starbucks developed a loyal following and established itself as a premium brand. As the company expanded, it maintained its focus on quality and customer experience, allowing it to grow into a global coffee giant.

3. **Etsy:** Etsy targeted the niche market of handmade and vintage goods, connecting independent crafters and artists with customers seeking unique, one-of-a-kind items. By focusing on this niche, Etsy differentiated itself from mass-market e-commerce platforms and built a strong community of loyal buyers and sellers.
4. **McDonald's:** In the early days, McDonald's targeted a niche market of busy, working-class Americans who wanted quick, affordable meals. By focusing on this niche and developing a standardized system for fast food production, McDonald's was able to offer consistent quality and value to its customers. As the company expanded, it maintained its core value proposition while adapting its menu to local tastes and preferences, enabling it to become a global fast-food icon.
5. **Warby Parker:** As mentioned earlier, Warby Parker initially focused on the niche of affordable, stylish eyewear for fashion-conscious consumers. By targeting this niche, the company was able to develop expertise in customer preferences, build a loyal following, and disrupt the traditional eyewear industry.
6. **Lululemon:** Lululemon initially targeted a niche market of yoga enthusiasts, offering high-quality, performance-oriented yoga apparel. By focusing on this niche and fostering a sense of community among its customers, Lululemon developed a loyal following and established itself as a premium brand in the athletic apparel industry. As the company expanded, it maintained its commitment to quality and customer experience, allowing it to grow into a global lifestyle brand.
7. **Tesla:** Tesla initially targeted a niche market of environmentally conscious, high-net-worth individuals who wanted a luxury electric vehicle. By focusing on this niche and developing innovative, high-performance electric cars, Tesla was able to establish itself as a leader in the electric vehicle industry. As the company has grown, it has expanded its product line to include more affordable models, catering to a broader audience while maintaining its focus on sustainability and innovation.

Expanding Beyond the Initial Niche

While targeting a niche market is crucial for early-stage brand growth, successful brands often expand beyond their initial niche over time. As brands build a loyal customer base and establish expertise in their niche, they can identify adjacent market opportunities and gradually broaden their target audience.

However, it's essential for brands to maintain their core value proposition and brand identity as they expand. By staying true to the unique qualities that resonated with their initial niche audience, brands can attract new customers while retaining the loyalty of their core base.

Strategies for expanding beyond the initial niche include:

1. **Product Line Expansion:** Brands can introduce new products or services that cater to the evolving needs of their target audience or adjacent market segments.
2. **Market Segmentation:** Brands can identify new customer segments that share similar needs or preferences to their initial niche and develop targeted offerings for these segments.
3. **Partnerships and Collaborations:** Brands can partner with other companies or influencers to reach new audiences and expand their market presence.
4. **Geographic Expansion:** Brands can expand into new geographic markets, leveraging their expertise and reputation to attract customers in different regions.

The Law of Niche emphasizes the importance of focusing on a specific target audience in the early stages of brand development. By concentrating resources on meeting the unique needs of a niche market, brands can differentiate themselves, build expertise, and foster a loyal customer base. This foundation sets the stage for future growth and expansion, allowing brands to gradually broaden their reach while staying true to their core value proposition.

***

4

The Law of Focus

In the world of branding, it's essential to understand that a brand should be known for one thing above all else. The Law of Focus states that a brand should initially concentrate on a single product, service, or concept, becoming synonymous with that offering in the minds of consumers. By focusing on one thing, a brand can establish a clear identity, differentiate itself from competitors, and build a strong foundation for future growth and expansion.

The importance of focus in branding cannot be overstated. In the words of marketing expert Al Ries, "A product for everybody is a product for nobody." When a brand tries to be everything to everyone, it risks diluting its message and failing to connect with any specific audience. On the other hand, when a brand focuses on a single offering and becomes known for it, it can create a powerful association in the minds of consumers, making it easier to attract and retain customers.

One classic example of the Law of Focus in action is Dial soap. When Dial first entered the market, it focused solely on producing antibacterial soap. By concentrating on this one product and emphasizing its unique antibacterial properties, Dial was able to establish itself as the go-to brand for consumers looking for a soap that could help protect against germs. The brand became so closely associated with antibacterial soap that "Dial" became synonymous with the product category itself.

Another example is Amazon. When Amazon first launched in 1994, it focused exclusively on selling books online. By concentrating on this one product category and providing a wide selection, competitive prices, and convenient delivery, Amazon was able to establish itself as the premier online destination for book lovers. As the company grew, it maintained its focus on books while gradually expanding into other product categories, such as music, movies, and electronics. By the time Amazon began offering a wider range of products, it had already built a strong reputation and loyal customer base, which helped it succeed in new markets.

The Law of Focus is particularly important for new and emerging brands. When a brand is just starting, it often has limited resources and must compete with established players in the market. By focusing on a single offering and becoming the best at delivering that product or service, a new brand can carve out a niche for itself and attract a dedicated following. This focused approach allows the brand to allocate its resources more effectively, develop deep expertise in its chosen area, and create a memorable brand identity.

To apply the Law of Focus in your own branding efforts, start by identifying the one thing you want your brand to be known for. This could be a specific product, service, or concept that sets you apart from competitors and resonates with your target audience. Once you've identified your focus, craft your brand messaging, visual identity, and marketing efforts around that central idea. Consistently communicate your focus across all touchpoints, from your website and social media to your packaging and customer service.

As your brand grows and establishes itself in the market, you can begin to expand into other product categories or service offerings. However, it's essential to maintain your core focus and ensure that any new offerings align with your brand's identity and values. By staying true to your focus, you can maintain the loyalty of your existing customers while attracting new ones who appreciate your brand's expertise and dedication.

Examples of brands that have successfully applied the Law of Focus include:

1. **Coca-Cola:** Originally focused on a single product, Coca-Cola has become synonymous with soft drinks worldwide.
2. **Nike:** Initially focused on running shoes, Nike has become a global leader in athletic footwear and apparel.
3. **Tesla:** By focusing on electric vehicles, Tesla has established itself as a leader in the automotive industry and a symbol of innovation and sustainability.
4. **Roku:** Roku initially focused on a single product – a streaming media player that allowed users to access content from various online platforms on their TVs. By concentrating on this one offering and providing a user-friendly interface and wide range of content options, Roku established itself as a leader in the streaming device market. As the company has grown, it has expanded into smart TVs and advertising services while maintaining its core focus on streaming.
5. **Slack:** Slack is a workplace communication platform that initially focused on solving a specific problem – reducing the reliance on email for internal communication. By concentrating on this one issue and developing a user-friendly, feature-rich platform, Slack quickly gained popularity among businesses and teams. As the company has grown, it has added new features and integrations while maintaining its core focus on streamlining workplace communication.
6. **Spanx:** Spanx started with a single product – footless pantyhose designed to smooth and shape a woman's silhouette. By focusing on this one offering and emphasizing its unique benefits, Spanx quickly gained a following among women looking for comfortable, effective shapewear. As the company has expanded, it has introduced new products, such as leggings and bras, while staying true to its core focus on shaping and smoothing.
7. **Square:** Square initially focused on a single product – a small, portable credit card reader that allowed small businesses to accept payments using their smartphones or tablets. By concentrating on this one offering and making it easy and affordable for businesses to accept credit card payments, Square quickly gained traction in the market. As the

company has grown, it has expanded into other financial services, such as invoicing and payroll processing, while maintaining its core focus on empowering small businesses.

In conclusion, the Law of Focus is a critical principle in building a strong, enduring brand. By concentrating on a single offering and becoming the best at delivering that product or service, brands can establish a clear identity, differentiate themselves from competitors, and build a loyal customer base. As you develop your own brand, remember to identify your focus, consistently communicate it across all touchpoints, and stay true to it as you grow and expand. By doing so, you'll create a brand that not only resonates with your target audience but also stands the test of time.

* * *

5

The Law of Positioning

In the crowded marketplace, where countless brands vie for consumers' attention, it's essential to understand the importance of positioning. The Law of Positioning states that a brand must find a clear, distinctive, and desirable place in the minds of its target audience relative to its competitors. In other words, positioning is about defining how you want your customers to perceive your brand and what unique value it offers compared to other options in the market.

The concept of positioning is rooted in the way the human mind works. From an evolutionary perspective, our brains are wired to categorize information to make sense of the world around us. This innate tendency to organize and store information in categories helps us process new data more efficiently and make decisions more quickly. When it comes to brands, consumers naturally associate them with specific categories, attributes, and benefits, forming a mental "positioning" for each brand they encounter.

To effectively position your brand, you must first understand what already exists in your target audience's minds. This includes identifying the categories they associate with your product or service, as well as the other brands that occupy those categories. By understanding the existing mental landscape, you can identify opportunities to differentiate your brand and carve out a unique position that sets you apart from competitors.

One of the most powerful ways to position a brand is to be the first in a new category. When a brand introduces a new product or service that doesn't fit neatly into existing categories, it has the opportunity to define the category and become the standard by which all future entrants are judged. This first-mover advantage can create a lasting association between the brand and the category in consumers' minds, making it difficult for competitors to dislodge the brand from its position.

Examples of brands that have successfully positioned themselves as category leaders include:

1. **Kleenex:** The brand name has become synonymous with facial tissues, to the point where many people use "Kleenex" as a generic term for the product.
2. **Band-Aid:** Similarly, Band-Aid has become the default term for adhesive bandages, even though there are many other brands in the market.
3. **Google:** Google has become so closely associated with online search that "googling" has become a verb, representing the act of searching for information online.

However, being the first in a category isn't always possible, especially in mature markets with established players. In these cases, brands must find other ways to differentiate themselves and claim a unique position in consumers' minds. This can involve emphasizing a specific attribute, benefit, or target audience that sets the brand apart from competitors.

For example, when Apple introduced the iPhone, it wasn't the first smartphone on the market. However, Apple positioned the iPhone as a revolutionary device that combined the functionality of a phone, music player, and internet communicator in one sleek, user-friendly package. By emphasizing design, ease of use, and a unique combination of features, Apple was able to carve out a distinctive position in the smartphone market and become a leader in the category.

Another approach to positioning is to be the second brand in a category, positioning yourself as the alternative to the category leader. This can be an effective strategy for brands that can't claim first-mover advantage but still want to establish a strong presence in the market. By positioning themselves as the "other" option, these brands can attract consumers who are looking for something different from the category leader.

Examples of brands that have successfully positioned themselves as alternatives include:

1. **Pepsi:** While Coca-Cola is the dominant brand in the cola category, Pepsi has positioned itself as the youthful, energetic alternative.
2. **Burger King:** In the fast-food hamburger category, McDonald's is the clear leader, but Burger King has positioned itself as the edgier, more rebellious option with its "Have It Your Way" slogan and marketing campaigns.

To apply the Law of Positioning to your own brand, start by conducting research to understand the existing mental landscape of your target audience. Identify the categories, attributes, and benefits they associate with your product or service, as well as the other brands that occupy those spaces. Look for opportunities to differentiate your brand and claim a unique position that sets you apart from competitors.

Once you've identified your desired position, develop a clear, consistent messaging strategy that communicates your brand's unique value proposition and reinforces your position in the market. This messaging should be reflected in all aspects of your brand, from your product design and packaging to your advertising and customer service.

It's important to note that positioning is an ongoing process, not a one-time event. As markets evolve and new competitors emerge, brands must continually reassess their position and make adjustments to stay relevant and differentiated in the minds of consumers.

A Few More Examples

1. **7 Up:** In the 1920s, the soft drink market was dominated by cola-based beverages like Coca-Cola and Pepsi. 7 Up saw an opportunity to differentiate itself by creating a new category of "un-cola" or "lemon-lime" soft drinks. By positioning itself as a refreshing alternative to colas, 7 Up was able to carve out a unique space in the market and become the leader in the lemon-lime soda category.
2. **Red Bull:** In the 1980s, Dietrich Mateschitz discovered a Thai energy drink called Krating Daeng, which inspired him to create Red Bull. At the time, there were no energy drinks in Western markets, and the concept was virtually unknown. Red Bull positioned itself as a unique product that could provide a boost of energy and mental alertness, creating an entirely new category in the beverage industry. By being the first and most prominent brand in the energy drink category, Red Bull has maintained a dominant position and inspired countless imitators.
3. **Gatorade:** Gatorade was developed in 1965 by researchers at the University of Florida to help the school's football team stay hydrated during games. At the time, there were no sports drinks on the market, and athletes relied on water to stay hydrated. Gatorade positioned itself as a scientifically formulated drink that could replenish electrolytes and provide energy to athletes, creating the sports drink category. As the first and most recognized brand in this new category, Gatorade has maintained a leadership position for decades.
4. **Starbucks:** Before Starbucks, coffee shops in the United States were primarily small, independent businesses that focused on providing a quick caffeine fix. Starbucks saw an opportunity to create a new category of coffee shops that offered a premium, customizable coffee experience in a comfortable, inviting atmosphere. By positioning itself as a "third place" between work and home where people could relax, socialize, and enjoy high-quality coffee, Starbucks created a new category and became the dominant brand in the specialty coffee market.
5. **Tesla:** When Tesla introduced its first electric car, the Roadster, in

2008, electric vehicles were seen as a niche product with limited appeal. Tesla positioned itself as a luxury brand that offered high-performance, environmentally friendly cars, creating a new category of premium electric vehicles. By focusing on design, performance, and innovation, Tesla has become the leader in the electric vehicle market and has forced traditional automakers to invest heavily in developing their own electric models.

In conclusion, the Law of Positioning is a critical principle for building a strong, enduring brand. By understanding the mental landscape of your target audience and carving out a unique, desirable position relative to competitors, you can create a powerful association between your brand and the value it offers. Whether you're the first in a new category or positioning yourself as an alternative to the category leader, a clear, consistent positioning strategy is essential for long-term success in the marketplace.

* * *

6

The Law of Differentiation

In today's crowded marketplace, where consumers are bombarded with countless options and messages, it's essential for brands to stand out from the competition. The Law of Differentiation states that a brand must have a clear, unique, and compelling difference that sets it apart from its competitors in the minds of its target audience. This differentiation can be based on a variety of factors, such as product features, quality, price, service, or emotional appeal.

The importance of differentiation lies in the fact that consumers are more likely to remember and choose brands that are distinct and relevant to their needs. When a brand blends in with its competitors, it becomes forgettable and interchangeable, making it difficult to attract and retain customers. On the other hand, when a brand has a clear, compelling point of difference, it gives consumers a reason to choose it over other options and helps build loyalty and advocacy over time.

To effectively differentiate your brand, you must first understand your target audience and what they value most in your product or service category. This requires deep insights into their needs, preferences, behaviours, and pain points, as well as an understanding of the competitive landscape. By identifying the key attributes and benefits that matter most to your target audience, you can develop a differentiation strategy that speaks directly to their desires and sets your brand apart from competitors.

There are several ways to differentiate a brand, depending on the nature of the product or service and the characteristics of the target audience. Some common approaches to differentiation include:

1. **Product features:** Offering unique or superior product features that address specific customer needs or preferences.
2. **Quality:** Providing higher quality products or services than competitors, often justified by a premium price.
3. **Price:** Offering the lowest price in the category, appealing to cost-conscious consumers.
4. **Service:** Delivering exceptional customer service or support that goes above and beyond what competitors offer.
5. **Emotional appeal:** Creating a strong emotional connection with customers through storytelling, values, or personality.
6. **Convenience:** Making the product or service more convenient or accessible than competitors.
7. **Expertise:** Demonstrating specialized knowledge or expertise in a particular area, establishing the brand as an authority.

Examples of brands that have successfully differentiated themselves include:

1. **Apple:** Apple has differentiated itself through a combination of innovative product design, user-friendly interfaces, and a strong emotional connection with customers. By creating products that are both functional and desirable, Apple has built a loyal fan base that sees the brand as a status symbol and a reflection of their personal style.
2. **Zappos:** Zappos, an online shoe and clothing retailer, has differentiated itself through exceptional customer service. By offering free shipping and returns, 24/7 customer support, and a 365-day return policy, Zappos has created a stress-free shopping experience that sets it apart from other online retailers.
3. **Patagonia:** Patagonia, an outdoor clothing and gear company, has differentiated itself through its commitment to environmental sustainability

and social responsibility. By using eco-friendly materials, donating a portion of its profits to environmental causes, and encouraging customers to buy only what they need, Patagonia has built a strong reputation as a purpose-driven brand that aligns with its customers' values.

4. **Tesla:** Tesla has differentiated itself in the automotive industry by focusing solely on electric vehicles and prioritizing innovation, performance, and sustainability. By creating a unique brand identity and customer experience centered around advanced technology and environmental responsibility, Tesla has attracted a loyal following of customers who are willing to pay a premium for its products.

5. **Airbnb:** Airbnb has differentiated itself from traditional hotels by offering a more personalized and authentic travel experience. By enabling travelers to stay in unique accommodations and connect with local hosts, Airbnb has created a differentiated value proposition that appeals to customers seeking a more immersive and memorable travel experience.

To apply the Law of Differentiation to your own brand, start by conducting a thorough analysis of your target audience and the competitive landscape. Identify the key attributes and benefits that matter most to your customers and look for opportunities to differentiate your brand based on those factors. Consider how you can create a unique and compelling value proposition that speaks directly to your target audience's needs and desires.

Once you've identified your brand's point of differentiation, develop a clear and consistent messaging strategy that communicates that difference across all touchpoints, from your product design and packaging to your advertising and customer service. Continuously reinforce your brand's unique value proposition through your actions and interactions with customers, building a strong and distinctive brand identity over time.

It's important to note that differentiation is an ongoing process, not a one-time event. As markets evolve and new competitors emerge, brands must continually reassess their points of differentiation and make adjustments to stay relevant and compelling to their target audience. This requires a deep understanding of customer needs and preferences, as well as a willingness to adapt and innovate in response to changing market conditions.

In conclusion, the Law of Differentiation is critical for building a strong, enduring brand in today's competitive marketplace. By identifying and communicating a clear, unique, and compelling point of difference, brands can attract and retain customers, build loyalty and advocacy, and establish a lasting competitive advantage. Whether through product features, quality, service, emotional appeal, or other factors, differentiation is essential for any brand that wants to stand out and succeed in the long run.

Now, let's discuss how the Law of Value Proposition, the Law of Focus, the Law of Positioning, and the Law of Differentiation work together to create a strong brand strategy.

The Law of Value Proposition is the foundation of a strong brand strategy. It defines the unique value that a brand offers to its target audience, based on a deep understanding of their needs, desires, and pain points. A clear and compelling value proposition sets the stage for the other laws to come into play.

The Law of Focus builds on the value proposition by identifying the one thing that a brand should be known for. By focusing on a single product, service, or concept, a brand can create a strong and memorable identity that differentiates it from competitors. This focus helps to reinforce the value proposition and make it more tangible and relevant to customers.

The Law of Positioning takes the value proposition and focus and uses them to create a distinct and desirable place for the brand in the minds of its target audience. Positioning involves understanding the competitive landscape and identifying opportunities to carve out a unique space that sets the brand apart from competitors. Effective positioning helps to reinforce the value proposition and focus, making the brand more memorable and compelling to customers.

Finally, the Law of Differentiation builds on the positioning by identifying the specific attributes, benefits, or qualities that make the brand unique and superior to competitors. Differentiation involves communicating the brand's unique value proposition and positioning through every touchpoint, from product design and packaging to advertising and customer service. By consistently reinforcing its differentiation, a brand can build a strong and enduring identity that resonates with its target audience.

While each of these laws plays a distinct role in creating a strong brand strategy, there is also significant overlap and interaction between them. For example, a brand's value proposition and focus often inform its positioning and differentiation, while its positioning and differentiation help to reinforce and communicate its value proposition and focus. Similarly, a brand's focus and differentiation may evolve as its value proposition and positioning shift in response to changing market conditions and customer needs.

Ultimately, the key to creating a strong brand strategy is to develop a clear and compelling value proposition, focus on a single core concept or offering, position the brand in a unique and desirable space in the minds of its target audience, and differentiate the brand through consistent and compelling communication and execution. By leveraging the power of these four laws and understanding their interaction and overlap, brands can create a strong and enduring identity that resonates with customers and drives long-term success.

* * *

7

The Law of Purpose

In today's socially conscious and values-driven marketplace, customers are increasingly looking to support brands that stand for something bigger than just making a profit. The Law of Purpose states that a brand must have a clear and compelling reason for being, beyond just selling products or services. This purpose should be authentic, meaningful, and aligned with the values and aspirations of the brand's target audience.

The importance of purpose lies in the fact that customers today are more informed, empowered, and discerning than ever before. They are looking for brands that not only meet their functional needs, but also resonate with their beliefs and contribute positively to society and the environment. Brands that lack a clear and authentic purpose risk being seen as shallow, opportunistic, or even irrelevant in the eyes of their customers.

Having a strong brand purpose can bring many benefits, including:

1. **Differentiation:** A compelling purpose can help a brand stand out in a crowded marketplace and give customers a reason to choose it over competitors.
2. **Loyalty:** Customers are more likely to form deep and lasting connections with brands that share their values and contribute to causes they care about.
3. **Advocacy:** When customers believe in a brand's purpose, they are more

likely to become brand advocates, recommending the brand to others and defending it against criticism.
4. **Employee engagement:** A strong purpose can also inspire and motivate employees, giving them a sense of meaning and fulfillment in their work.
5. **Innovation:** A clear purpose can guide a brand's innovation efforts, helping it to develop products, services, and experiences that are truly meaningful and relevant to its customers.

To develop a strong brand purpose, companies must start by looking inward and identifying the core values, beliefs, and aspirations that drive their business. This requires honest introspection and a willingness to look beyond short-term profits to consider the broader impact and legacy of the brand.

Once a brand has identified its core purpose, it must find authentic and meaningful ways to bring that purpose to life through its products, services, and interactions with customers. This may involve:

1. Developing products or services that address social or environmental challenges.
2. Partnering with non-profit organizations or causes that align with the brand's purpose.
3. Incorporating sustainable and ethical practices into the brand's supply chain and operations.
4. Engaging customers in meaningful conversations and initiatives around the brand's purpose.
5. Empowering employees to be ambassadors and advocates for the brand's purpose.

It's important to note that a brand's purpose must be authentic and consistently demonstrated through actions, not just words. Customers are quick to spot inconsistencies or "purpose-washing," where a brand claims to have a purpose but fails to live up to it in practice.

Examples of brands with strong and authentic purposes include:

1. **Patagonia:** Patagonia's purpose is to "use business to inspire and implement solutions to the environmental crisis." The brand consistently demonstrates this purpose through its use of sustainable materials, its advocacy for environmental causes, and its commitment to donating 1% of sales to environmental organizations.
2. **McDonald's:** McDonald's purpose is to "feed and foster communities." While primarily known for its fast food, McDonald's also demonstrates its commitment to communities through initiatives like Ronald McDonald House Charities, which provides housing for families near hospitals where their children are receiving treatment. McDonald's also invests in education and youth sports programs in the communities it serves.
3. **Ben & Jerry's:** Ben & Jerry's purpose is to "make the best possible ice cream in the nicest possible way." The brand is known for its commitment to social justice, environmental sustainability, and ethical sourcing, and regularly uses its platform to advocate for causes aligned with its values.
4. **Starbucks:** Starbucks' purpose is to "inspire and nurture the human spirit – one person, one cup, and one neighborhood at a time." The brand brings this purpose to life through its commitment to ethical sourcing of coffee, its investment in employee education and well-being, and its efforts to create welcoming "third place" environments in its stores. Starbucks also regularly engages in social and environmental initiatives, such as its commitment to hiring refugees and veterans.
5. **Amazon:** Amazon's purpose is to "be Earth's most customer-centric company." While this purpose may seem broad, Amazon demonstrates it through its relentless focus on innovation, convenience, and customer satisfaction. From its personalized product recommendations to its fast and reliable delivery, Amazon constantly strives to anticipate and meet the evolving needs of its customers.
6. **Nike:** Nike's purpose is to "bring inspiration and innovation to every athlete* in the world." The brand's famous asterisk adds, "If you have a body, you are an athlete." This inclusive purpose has guided Nike's efforts to create innovative athletic products, support athlete

communities, and inspire people to push their limits. Nike also uses its platform to advocate for social causes, such as racial equality and LGBTQ+ rights.

7. **Spotify:** Spotify's purpose is to "unlock the potential of human creativity by giving a million creative artists the opportunity to live off their art and billions of fans the opportunity to enjoy and be inspired by it." The brand brings this purpose to life through its music streaming platform, which uses data and algorithms to connect listeners with new and relevant artists. Spotify also invests in tools and resources to help artists grow their careers and reach new audiences.

In conclusion, the Law of Purpose is a critical principle for building a strong, enduring, and impactful brand in today's values-driven marketplace. By having a clear and authentic reason for being, beyond just making a profit, brands can differentiate themselves, inspire loyalty and advocacy, and contribute positively to society and the environment. Developing and living up to a strong brand purpose requires introspection, authenticity, and consistency, but the rewards – for both the brand and the world – can be significant.

* * *

8

The Law of Authenticity

In a world where consumers are bombarded with countless marketing messages and brand promises, authenticity has become a rare and valuable currency. The Law of Authenticity states that a brand must be genuine, consistent, and true to its core values and purpose. Authenticity is about more than just honesty; it's about having a clear identity and living up to it in every interaction with customers.

The importance of authenticity lies in the fact that today's consumers are more savvy and skeptical than ever before. They have access to vast amounts of information about brands, and they can quickly spot inconsistencies or false promises. Brands that lack authenticity risk being seen as untrustworthy, insincere, or even manipulative.

On the other hand, brands that consistently demonstrate authenticity can build deep and lasting relationships with their customers. When a brand is true to its values and delivers on its promises, customers are more likely to trust it, respect it, and become loyal advocates for it.

Authenticity is closely linked to the Law of Purpose, as discussed in the previous chapter. A brand's purpose is the foundation of its authenticity – it defines the brand's core reason for being and guides its actions and decisions. To cultivate authenticity, brands must start by clearly defining their core values, mission, and purpose through introspection and honesty. Once these core elements are established, the brand must consistently express and embody them through every touchpoint and interaction with customers.

Consistency is key to authenticity. Brands must ensure that their messaging, products, services, and customer experiences all align with their core identity. This means using high-quality ingredients, sustainable materials, or traditional craftsmanship methods that reflect the brand's values and purpose. Brands should also be transparent about their processes and sourcing, and be willing to share this information with customers.

Authentic communication should feel genuine, relatable, and true to the brand's core identity. Gimmicks or insincere marketing tactics should be avoided in favor of building meaningful connections with customers through honest and engaging content. Brands should be upfront about their strengths and weaknesses, successes and failures, and be willing to admit mistakes and take responsibility for them.

Authenticity also involves staying true to the brand's roots and heritage. Brands with a strong sense of history and tradition can leverage this as a powerful source of authenticity. By celebrating their origins and staying connected to their foundational values, these brands can maintain a sense of timelessness and reliability that resonates with customers.

However, it's important to note that authenticity is not a one-time achievement, but an ongoing commitment. Brands must continually strive to live up to their purpose and values, even as they grow and evolve over time. Inconsistencies or contradictions can quickly erode a brand's authenticity and trust with customers.

Chobani Yogurt is a great example of a brand that has consistently demonstrated authenticity in its journey to becoming a leading yogurt brand in the United States.

Chobani's founder, Hamdi Ulukaya, is a Turkish immigrant who grew up in a dairy-farming family. When he bought a defunct yogurt factory in upstate New York, his goal was to bring the authentic taste and quality of Mediterranean-style yogurt to American consumers.

From the start, Chobani has been committed to using simple, natural ingredients and traditional yogurt-making methods. The company sources its milk from local farms and uses a straining process to remove excess water, resulting in a thicker, creamier yogurt. Chobani has been transparent about its ingredients and processes, even inviting customers to visit its factories and see how the yogurt is made.

Chobani's commitment to authenticity extends beyond its products. The company has a strong sense of social responsibility and has made efforts to support the communities in which it operates. Chobani has donated a portion of its profits to charity, provided yogurt to schools and food banks, and offered job opportunities to refugees and immigrants.

In its marketing and communication, Chobani has maintained an authentic and relatable voice. The brand's advertising often features real people and their stories, rather than celebrity endorsements or staged scenarios. Chobani has also been quick to respond to customer feedback and concerns, demonstrating a genuine commitment to transparency and accountability.

Another example of a brand that has demonstrated authenticity is Moleskine. Moleskine is an Italian company that produces high-quality notebooks, journals, and other stationery products.

The Moleskine brand is rooted in a rich history and cultural tradition. The company's notebooks are inspired by the simple, black notebooks used by famous artists and writers like Vincent van Gogh, Pablo Picasso, and Ernest Hemingway. By connecting its products to this creative heritage, Moleskine has established a sense of authenticity and timelessness.

Moleskine's commitment to quality and craftsmanship is another key aspect of its authenticity. The company uses premium materials, such as acid-free paper and durable covers, to create products that are built to last. Moleskine's minimalist design and attention to detail also contribute to its authentic brand identity.

In its marketing and communication, Moleskine celebrates the creativity and self-expression of its customers. The brand's social media channels and website feature customer artwork and stories, showcasing how people use Moleskine products to capture their ideas and experiences. This user-generated content feels authentic and reinforces Moleskine's connection to its creative community.

In summary, authenticity is rooted in a brand's purpose and values and is maintained through consistent expression, transparent communication, and a strong connection to the brand's heritage. By prioritizing authenticity, brands can build lasting relationships with customers based on trust, credibility, and shared values.

* * *

III

Part 03—Brand Identity

9

The Law of Simplicity

In the world of branding, simplicity is a powerful tool that can help businesses cut through the noise and connect with their target audience. The Law of Simplicity states that the most effective brands are those that can communicate their core message and values in a clear, concise, and easily understandable manner.

Simplicity in branding is about stripping away the unnecessary complexities and focusing on the essential elements that define your brand. This applies to all aspects of your brand, from your logo and visual identity to your messaging and customer experience.

Here are some key reasons why simplicity is crucial in branding:

1. **Clarity:** A simple brand message is easier for customers to understand and remember. When your brand is clear and straightforward, it reduces confusion and helps people quickly grasp what you stand for and what you offer.
2. **Memorability:** Simple brands are more memorable. When your brand elements, such as your logo, tagline, and messaging, are simple and consistent, they are more likely to stick in people's minds and create a lasting impression.
3. **Differentiation:** In a crowded market, simplicity can help your brand stand out. By focusing on a single, clear message or value proposition,

you can differentiate yourself from competitors who may be trying to communicate too many things at once.
4. **Versatility:** Simple brands are more adaptable and can be applied across various media and contexts. A simple logo, for example, can be easily recognized whether it appears on a billboard, a social media post, or a product package.
5. **Timelessness:** Simple brands tend to have a more timeless quality, as they are less likely to be tied to passing trends or fads. This means that a simple brand can remain relevant and effective for years or even decades.

To apply the Law of Simplicity to your brand, consider the following:

1. **Identify your core message:** What is the single most important thing you want your customers to know about your brand? Focus on communicating this message clearly and consistently.
2. **Simplify your visual identity:** Choose a simple, memorable logo and color scheme that can be easily recognized and reproduced across different media.
3. **Use plain language:** Avoid jargon or overly complex language in your brand messaging. Use clear, concise language that is easy for your target audience to understand.
4. **Streamline your offerings:** Instead of trying to be everything to everyone, focus on doing a few things exceptionally well. This will make it easier for customers to understand what your brand is all about.
5. **Ensure consistency:** Consistency is key to simplicity. Ensure that your brand elements, messaging, and customer experience are consistent across all touchpoints.

Apple

Apple is a prime example of a brand that embraces simplicity in every aspect of its business. From its products to its marketing and retail experiences, Apple consistently delivers a clear, streamlined message.

Clean lines, intuitive interfaces, and a focus on user experience characterize Apple's product design. The company's iconic logo, an apple with a bite taken out of it, is simple, memorable, and easily recognizable. Apple's packaging is also minimalistic, with a focus on showcasing the product itself.

In its marketing, Apple often uses simple, bold imagery and messaging that focuses on the benefits of its products rather than technical specifications. Its "Think Different" campaign, for example, featured black and white photographs of iconic figures and a simple, powerful message about the importance of creativity and innovation.

Apple's retail stores also embody simplicity, with open, uncluttered spaces, minimal signage, and a focus on product displays. The company's Genius Bar offers a straightforward, personalized approach to customer service.

By consistently applying the Law of Simplicity across its business, Apple has built a strong, memorable brand that resonates with customers around the world.

Trader Joe's

Trader Joe's, a grocery store chain, has built a loyal following by embracing simplicity in its product offerings, store design, and customer experience.

Unlike many grocery stores that offer a wide variety of brands and products, Trader Joe's focuses on a curated selection of high-quality, unique items, many of which are sold under its own private label. This simplifies the shopping experience for customers and helps Trader Joe's differentiate itself from competitors.

Trader Joe's stores are also designed with simplicity in mind. The company uses a consistent, straightforward layout that makes it easy for customers to navigate and find what they need. Signage is clear and often incorporates playful, conversational language that reflects the brand's friendly, laid-back personality.

Trader Joe's also simplifies the customer experience by offering friendly, knowledgeable staff who are eager to assist shoppers and offer product recommendations. The company's "Fearless Flyer" newsletter features simple, engaging descriptions of featured products, often with a quirky, humorous tone.

By focusing on a curated product selection, straightforward store design, and a simple, friendly customer experience, Trader Joe's has built a strong, differentiated brand that has earned a dedicated following.

Dropbox

Dropbox, a cloud storage and file sharing service, has built a strong brand by focusing on simplicity in terms of its product's functionality and user experience.

When Dropbox first launched, cloud storage was a relatively new concept for many users. The company succeeded by making its product incredibly easy to understand and use. Its core message was simple: Dropbox is a place to keep all your files safe, synced, and easy to share.

Dropbox's interface is designed to be intuitive and straightforward, with a focus on the core actions of storing, syncing, and sharing files. The company has consistently resisted the temptation to add too many bells and whistles, instead focusing on refining its core product and making it as reliable and user-friendly as possible.

In its marketing, Dropbox often uses clear, concise language and imagery that reinforces the simplicity and ease of use of its product. By maintaining this focus on simplicity, Dropbox has built a strong, trusted brand in a competitive market.

Warby Parker

Warby Parker, an eyewear retailer, has disrupted its industry by offering a simple, customer-centric approach to buying glasses.

Traditionally, buying glasses was a complex process that involved visiting a store, trying on dozens of frames, and navigating a confusing array of lens options and add-ons. Warby Parker simplifies this process by offering a curated selection of stylish, high-quality frames at a straightforward price point.

The company's Home Try-On program, which allows customers to select up to five frames to try on at home for free, further simplifies the buying process. Warby Parker's website is easy to navigate, with clear, detailed product descriptions and a virtual try-on feature that helps customers visualize how frames will look on their face.

In its marketing and branding, Warby Parker uses a friendly, approachable tone and imagery that reflects its commitment to simplicity and customer service. The company's "Buy a Pair, Give a Pair" program, which donates a pair of glasses to someone in need for every pair purchased, also aligns with its simple, socially conscious brand identity.

By simplifying the process of buying glasses and offering a clear, customer-centric value proposition, Warby Parker has built a strong, disruptive brand in a traditional industry.

In conclusion, the Law of Simplicity is a critical principle for building a strong, effective brand. By focusing on clarity, memorability, differentiation, versatility, and timelessness, you can create a brand that resonates with your target audience and stands the test of time. Remember, in branding, less is often more.

* * *

10

The Law of Personality

In the world of branding, creating a strong, distinctive personality is essential for building a memorable and engaging brand. The Law of Personality states that brands should have a unique, recognizable character that resonates with their target audience and sets them apart from competitors.

A brand's personality is the set of human characteristics, emotions, and attributes that consumers associate with the brand. It encompasses the way a brand communicates, the values it represents, and the overall impression it leaves on its audience.

Here are some key reasons why having a strong brand personality is important:

1. **Differentiation:** In a crowded marketplace, a distinct brand personality can help you stand out from competitors and create a unique position in the minds of consumers.
2. **Emotional connection:** A well-defined brand personality allows consumers to form an emotional connection with your brand. People are more likely to engage with and remain loyal to brands that they can relate to on a personal level.
3. **Consistency:** A clear brand personality provides a framework for

consistent communication and behaviour across all touchpoints, from advertising and social media to customer service and product design.
4. **Memorability:** A strong, distinctive brand personality is more likely to stick in people's minds, making your brand more memorable and easily recognizable.
5. **Trust and loyalty:** When a brand has a consistent, authentic personality, it can help build trust and loyalty among consumers as they come to know what to expect from the brand.

To develop a strong brand personality, consider the following steps:

1. **Understand your target audience:** To create a brand personality that resonates, start by gaining a deep understanding of your target audience. Go beyond demographics and consider their psychographics, such as their values, interests, lifestyle, and aspirations. Engage with them through surveys, focus groups, and social media to learn what they seek in a brand.
2. **Identify your customers' desired brand traits:** Based on your target audience research, identify the key personality traits and attributes that your customers want to see in a brand within your product or service category. For example, if you're targeting busy young professionals, they may desire a brand that is efficient, reliable, and innovative.
3. **Align your brand's core values with customer preferences:** Ensure that your brand's core values align with the personality traits your target audience seeks. If your customers want a brand that is friendly and approachable, your core values should reflect empathy, inclusivity, and warmth. Use these values as the foundation for developing your brand personality.
4. **Develop a customer-centric brand voice:** Craft your brand's communication style and tone to match your target audience's preferences. If your customers prefer a friendly and approachable brand, use a conversational, relatable tone in your messaging. Ensure that your vocabulary, humor, and storytelling style resonate with your audience

and convey the desired personality traits.
5. **Maintain consistency across touchpoints:** Consistently express your brand's personality across all customer interactions, from your website and social media to your packaging and customer service. This consistency helps reinforce your brand's personality and builds trust with your target audience.
6. **Use storytelling to showcase your brand's personality:** Engage your audience by using storytelling techniques that highlight your brand's personality and values. Share narratives, anecdotes, and examples that illustrate how your brand embodies the traits your customers seek, such as friendliness, reliability, or innovation.
7. **Adapt to your audience's evolving needs:** As your target audience's preferences and expectations change over time, be prepared to adjust your brand's personality accordingly. Regularly engage with your customers to stay attuned to their evolving needs and ensure that your brand's personality continues to resonate with them.

Remember, your brand's personality should be an authentic reflection of the traits and values your customers seek in a brand within your specific product or service context.

Dollar Shave Club

Dollar Shave Club, a subscription-based razor and grooming products company, has built a brand personality that resonates with its target audience of young, budget-conscious men who appreciate convenience and humour.

Understanding that its customers desired a brand that was relatable, honest, and didn't take itself too seriously, Dollar Shave Club developed a personality that is witty, irreverent, and down-to-earth. This personality is consistently reflected across all touchpoints, from its website and product packaging to its viral video marketing campaigns.

The brand's voice is conversational, humorous, and often pokes fun at the traditional, overly serious tone of the men's grooming industry. Its famous launch video, "Our Blades Are F***ing Great," showcased the brand's personality by using deadpan humor and a straightforward, no-nonsense approach to discussing its products and value proposition.

Dollar Shave Club's packaging and product names also reflect its playful personality, with razor blades named "The Humble Twin" and "The 4X." The brand's social media presence maintains this tone, regularly engaging with customers using memes, jokes, and relatable content.

By crafting a brand personality that aligns with its target audience's desire for a relatable, humorous, and convenient grooming brand, Dollar Shave Club has built a strong, loyal customer base and disrupted the traditional men's razor industry.

Anthropologie

Anthropologie, a women's clothing, accessories, and home decor retailer, has cultivated a brand personality that resonates with its target audience of creative, affluent women who value unique, bohemian-inspired style.

Recognizing that its customers desired a brand that was artistic, worldly, and emotionally engaging, Anthropologie has developed a personality that is whimsical, aspirational, and slightly unconventional. This personality is consistently expressed through its product offerings, store design, and marketing communications.

Anthropologie's stores are designed to feel like immersive, discovery-driven experiences, with eclectic visual merchandising, custom art installations, and carefully curated product displays. Its product offerings often feature unique, limited-edition items sourced from artisans around the world, reinforcing the brand's worldly, one-of-a-kind personality.

The brand's marketing campaigns and catalogues showcase aspirational, bohemian-inspired imagery and storytelling that transport customers into the Anthropologie lifestyle. Its social media presence maintains this dreamy, artistic aesthetic, featuring user-generated content and engaging with customers through shared creativity and inspiration.

Anthropologie's brand voice is poetic, evocative, and often uses storytelling to create emotional connections with customers. Product descriptions are detailed and imaginative, painting a picture of the item's unique qualities and the feelings it evokes.

By consistently expressing a brand personality that aligns with its target audience's desire for a creative, aspirational, and emotionally engaging retail experience, Anthropologie has built a strong, loyal following and established itself as a destination for unique, bohemian-inspired style.

Yellow Tail

Yellow Tail has crafted a brand personality that resonates with its target audience of casual, unpretentious wine drinkers who value simplicity, fun, and accessibility. The brand's personality is friendly, laid-back, and adventurous, with a focus on enjoying life's simple pleasures.

1. **Approachable and unpretentious:** Yellow Tail's brand personality is designed to make wine feel accessible and unintimidating. The brand's messaging often emphasizes the idea that wine should be easy to understand and enjoy, without the need for extensive knowledge or expertise. This approachable personality is reflected in the brand's simple, colourful packaging and its straightforward product names, such as "Shiraz," "Chardonnay," and "Merlot."
2. **Fun and playful:** Yellow Tail's personality is fun-loving and playful, with a focus on the social, celebratory aspects of wine drinking. The brand's marketing campaigns often feature bright, bold colors, whimsical illustrations, and lighthearted messaging that encourages customers to "embrace the fun" and "let their taste buds dance." This playful personality is also reflected in the brand's signature yellow-footed wallaby logo, which adds a touch of whimsy and irreverence to the brand.
3. **Adventurous and free-spirited:** Yellow Tail's brand personality taps

into its customers' desire for exploration, spontaneity, and new experiences. The brand's marketing often features images of outdoor gatherings, exotic locations, and impromptu adventures, suggesting that Yellow Tail is the perfect companion for a free-spirited, exploratory lifestyle. This adventurous personality is also reflected in the brand's wide range of varietal wines, which encourage customers to explore different flavours and styles.

4. **Consistent brand voice:** Yellow Tail's brand voice is casual, friendly, and often incorporates playful, conversational language. The brand's website and social media presence maintain this laid-back, approachable tone, with engaging content that focuses on the social, fun-loving aspects of wine drinking. Product descriptions are straightforward and easy to understand, emphasizing taste and enjoyment over technical details or complex terminology.

5. **Customer-centric storytelling:** Yellow Tail's brand storytelling focuses on the experiences and emotions that resonate with its target audience. The brand's marketing often features relatable scenarios and characters, such as friends enjoying a casual outdoor gathering or a couple exploring a new city, with Yellow Tail as the perfect accompaniment to these moments. By showcasing these customer-centric stories, Yellow Tail reinforces its personality as a brand that understands and celebrates its customers' lifestyles and values.

By consistently expressing a brand personality that is approachable, fun-loving, and adventurous, Yellow Tail has successfully positioned itself as a go-to choice for casual, unpretentious wine drinkers.

In conclusion, the Law of Personality underscores the importance of creating a unique, recognizable brand character that resonates with your target audience. By developing a consistent, authentic personality, you can differentiate your brand, build emotional connections with consumers, and foster long-term trust and loyalty.

THE TIMELESS LAWS OF BRANDING

* * *

11

The Law of Voice & Tone

In the world of branding, the way a company communicates with its audience is just as important as the messages it conveys. The Law of Voice & Tone states that a brand's communication style should be consistent, distinctive, and reflective of its personality, values, and target audience.

A brand's voice is its unique personality and style of communication, while its tone refers to the emotional inflection and attitude expressed in its messaging. Together, voice and tone help create a recognizable, memorable, and emotionally resonant brand identity.

Here are some key reasons why having a consistent, distinctive voice and tone is crucial for brand success:

1. **Brand recognition:** A consistent voice and tone across all communications helps audiences easily recognize and remember your brand, even in a crowded market.
2. **Emotional connection:** By using a voice and tone that resonate with your target audience, you can create a deeper emotional connection and build stronger relationships with your customers.
3. **Trust and credibility:** Consistency in voice and tone helps establish trust and credibility, as it demonstrates that your brand is reliable, authentic, and true to its values.

4. **Differentiation:** A distinctive voice and tone can set your brand apart from competitors, making it easier for audiences to understand what makes your brand unique and why they should choose you.
5. **Engagement:** An engaging, relatable voice and tone can encourage audience interaction and participation, fostering a sense of community and loyalty around your brand.

To develop a strong brand voice and tone, consider the following steps:

1. **Define your brand personality:** Your voice and tone should be an extension of your brand's personality. Consider the human characteristics, emotions, and attributes you want your brand to embody, such as friendliness, sophistication, or quirkiness.
2. **Know your target audience:** Understand the communication styles, preferences, and expectations of your target audience. Your voice and tone should resonate with and appeal to the people you want to reach.
3. **Identify your brand's values and mission:** Your voice and tone should align with and support your brand's core values and mission. Consider how your communication style can reinforce your brand's purpose and positioning.
4. **Develop a brand voice guide:** Create a set of guidelines that define your brand's voice and tone, including specific characteristics, do's and don'ts, and examples of how to apply them across different types of content and channels.
5. **Ensure consistency:** Make sure all your brand communications, from website copy and social media posts to advertising and customer service interactions, consistently use your established voice and tone.
6. **Adapt to context:** While maintaining consistency, allow for some flexibility in tone based on the context and purpose of the communication. For example, a more serious tone may be appropriate for a crisis response, while a lighthearted tone may work better for a social media post.

Examples of brands with strong, distinctive voices and tones include:

1. **Mailchimp:** Mailchimp's voice is friendly, accessible, and slightly quirky, with a tone that is encouraging, empathetic, and playful. This approachable style helps the brand connect with small businesses and entrepreneurs.
2. **Nike:** Nike's voice is inspiring, confident, and bold, with a tone that is empowering, motivating, and sometimes provocative. This communication style reinforces the brand's mission to inspire athletes and encourage personal achievement.
3. **Slack:** Slack's voice is conversational, straightforward, and human, with a tone that is friendly, helpful, and occasionally humorous. This approachable style reflects the brand's mission to make work communication more efficient and enjoyable.

Old Spice

Old Spice, a men's grooming brand, has crafted a voice that is humorous, confident, and slightly over-the-top, with a tone that is playful, irreverent, and masculine. This communication style reflects the brand's personality as a fun, bold, and unapologetically manly choice for personal care products.

Old Spice's voice and tone are consistently expressed across its various marketing campaigns, product packaging, and social media interactions. The brand's advertising often features exaggerated, tongue-in-cheek scenarios that play on traditional masculine stereotypes, such as "The Man Your Man Could Smell Like" campaign, which features a suave, confident spokesman delivering rapid-fire, absurdist monologues about the brand's products.

Old Spice's product packaging and names also reflect its humorous, masculine voice, with names like "Swagger" and "Bearglove" and descriptions that use playful, hyperbolic language. The brand's social media presence maintains this voice and tone, with engaging, often ridiculous posts that encourage followers to embrace their manliness and have fun with grooming.

By consistently using a voice and tone that is entertaining, relatable, and aligned with its target audience's preferences, Old Spice has created a strong, memorable brand identity that stands out in the men's grooming market and fosters a loyal, engaged customer base.

Innocent Drinks

Innocent Drinks, a UK-based smoothie and juice company, has developed a voice that is friendly, casual, and slightly quirky, with a tone that is upbeat, optimistic, and socially conscious. This communication style reflects the brand's personality as a fun, approachable, and ethically-minded choice for healthy beverages.

Innocent's voice and tone are consistently expressed across its product packaging, website, and social media interactions. The brand's packaging features simple, colorful designs with playful, conversational copy that often includes jokes, puns, and whimsical illustrations. For example, a smoothie label might read, "We've crammed 75 raspberries into this bottle, along with a bunch of other delicious fruit. It's like a party in your mouth, but without the awkward small talk."

Innocent's website and social media presence maintain this friendly, informal voice and tone, with engaging content that often revolves around the brand's commitment to sustainability, healthy living, and social responsibility. The brand's "Daily Thoughts" on its website offer uplifting, humorous messages that reinforce its positive, optimistic tone.

Innocent's voice and tone also extend to its customer service interactions, with representatives who are trained to communicate in the same friendly, helpful manner. This consistency helps create a seamless, authentic brand experience that resonates with customers and reinforces Innocent's position as a likable, trustworthy brand.

By consistently using a voice and tone that is warm, engaging, and reflective of its core values, Innocent Drinks has created a strong, differentiated brand identity in the competitive beverage market.

The Law of Personality vs The Law of Voice & Tone

The Law of Personality focuses on the overall character and human-like attributes of a brand. It encompasses the emotional, psychological, and associative aspects that define a brand's identity and make it relatable to its target audience. A brand's personality is the set of traits, values, and qualities that consumers perceive and connect with, such as being friendly, sophisticated, or adventurous.

On the other hand, the Law of Voice & Tone specifically focuses on how a brand communicates and expresses its personality through language, both written and spoken. Voice refers to the consistent, recognizable style and character of a brand's communication, while the tone is the emotional inflexion and attitude adapted to different contexts and audiences.

In essence, the Law of Personality defines who a brand is, while the Law of Voice & Tone dictates how that brand personality is consistently communicated and expressed through language.

Here's a quick example to illustrate the difference:

Brand: Nike,

Personality: Inspiring, competitive, determined, and empowering.

Voice & Tone: Confident, motivating, and bold, with a tone that is encouraging and challenging.

While Nike's personality traits define its overall character, its voice and tone guide how the brand communicates that personality across various touchpoints, from advertising slogans to social media interactions.

In summary, the Law of Personality and the Law of Voice & Tone are closely related but distinct aspects of branding. A strong brand personality lays the foundation for a consistent and recognizable voice and tone, which in turn helps reinforce and communicate that personality to the target audience.

In conclusion, the Law of Voice & Tone emphasizes the importance of developing a consistent, distinctive communication style that reflects your brand's personality, values, and target audience. By crafting a strong voice and tone, you can create a memorable, emotionally resonant brand identity that sets you apart from competitors and fosters deeper connections with your customers.

* * *

12

The Law of Storytelling

In branding, the Law of Storytelling emphasizes the power of narrative in creating meaningful, memorable, and emotionally resonant connections with audiences. This law asserts that brands that effectively use storytelling to communicate their identity, values, and purpose are more likely to engage, inspire, and retain their target audience.

Storytelling is a fundamental human experience that has been used for centuries to share knowledge, entertain, and create emotional bonds. In the context of branding, storytelling involves crafting and sharing narratives that communicate a brand's unique identity, history, mission, and values in a way that resonates with its target audience.

Here are some key reasons why storytelling is a powerful tool for building strong, successful brands:

1. **Emotional connection:** Stories have the ability to evoke emotions and create deep, lasting connections with audiences. By sharing authentic, relatable stories, brands can tap into the emotions of their target audience and foster a sense of empathy, trust, and loyalty.
2. **Memorability:** People are more likely to remember information when it is presented in the form of a story. By embedding key brand messages and values into compelling narratives, brands can increase the likelihood that their audience will retain and recall that information over time.

3. **Differentiation:** In a crowded marketplace, storytelling can help brands differentiate themselves from competitors by highlighting their unique history, personality, and purpose. A well-crafted brand story can make a brand more memorable, recognizable, and appealing to its target audience.
4. **Authenticity:** Storytelling allows brands to showcase their authentic, human side and share their genuine passion, purpose, and values. By being transparent and true to their core identity, brands can build trust and credibility with their audience.
5. **Engagement:** Stories have the power to capture attention, spark curiosity, and encourage engagement. By sharing compelling narratives across various touchpoints, brands can encourage their audience to actively participate in and share their story, creating a sense of community and advocacy.

To effectively use storytelling in branding, consider the following tips:

1. **Define your brand's core story:** Identify the key elements of your brand's identity, including its history, mission, values, and purpose. These elements should form the foundation of your brand's core story.
2. **Know your audience:** Understand the needs, preferences, and values of your target audience. Your brand story should be crafted in a way that resonates with and appeals to the people you want to reach.
3. **Use a consistent narrative structure:** Ensure that your brand story follows a clear, consistent narrative structure across all touchpoints. This may include elements such as characters, conflict, and resolution.
4. **Evoke emotions:** Use storytelling techniques that evoke emotions and create a deep, lasting connection with your audience. This may include the use of humor, suspense, or inspiration.
5. **Integrate storytelling across touchpoints:** Incorporate your brand story across various touchpoints, such as your website, social media, advertising, and customer interactions. Consistency in storytelling helps reinforce your brand identity and message.

6. **Encourage audience participation:** Invite your audience to be a part of your brand story by encouraging them to share their own experiences, opinions, and stories related to your brand. This can create a sense of community and advocacy around your brand.

Johnnie Walker

Johnnie Walker, a Scottish whisky brand, has a rich history dating back to 1820. The brand's storytelling revolves around the theme of progress and personal journey, as embodied by its iconic "Striding Man" logo and the slogan "Keep Walking."

Johnnie Walker's brand story is deeply rooted in its heritage and the vision of its founder, John Walker, who started selling whisky in his small grocery store and eventually built a global brand. The brand's website features a detailed timeline that chronicles the key milestones and innovations in Johnnie Walker's history, from the introduction of the square bottle to the launch of its premium Blue Label blend.

The brand's "Keep Walking" slogan and "Striding Man" logo serve as powerful storytelling devices that symbolize progress, determination, and the pursuit of excellence. These elements are consistently featured across Johnnie Walker's advertising campaigns, product packaging, and promotional materials, reinforcing the brand's core narrative.

Johnnie Walker also uses storytelling to highlight the craftsmanship and quality of its products. The brand's website features detailed information about the whisky-making process, the unique characteristics of each blend, and the expert blenders behind the scenes. These stories help create a sense of authenticity and appreciation for the brand's commitment to its craft.

In addition, Johnnie Walker has released several short films and documentaries that showcase inspiring stories of progress and achievement from around the world. These storytelling initiatives not only reinforce the brand's core values but also create an emotional connection with its target audience by celebrating shared human experiences and aspirations.

By consistently telling its story of progress and craftsmanship across multiple touchpoints, Johnnie Walker has built a strong, compelling brand identity that resonates with its target audience and sets it apart in the competitive spirits industry.

TOMS Shoes

TOMS Shoes, a footwear and accessories company, has built its brand around the powerful story of "One for One." The company's narrative centers on the idea that for every pair of shoes purchased, TOMS donates a pair to a child in need. This story not only highlights the brand's commitment to social responsibility but also creates an emotional connection with its target audience.

TOMS' storytelling is integrated across various touchpoints, from its website and social media to its product packaging and in-store displays. The brand's website features a dedicated "Impact" section that shares stories and photos of the children and communities positively affected by TOMS' donations. These stories help customers see the tangible impact of their purchases and feel more emotionally invested in the brand.

TOMS also encourages its customers to be a part of its story by sharing their own experiences and photos with the brand's products using the hashtag #withTOMS. This user-generated content helps create a sense of community and advocacy around the brand, as customers feel like they are part of a larger movement to make a difference.

Furthermore, TOMS' annual "One Day Without Shoes" campaign invites people to go barefoot for a day to raise awareness for children's health and education. This experiential storytelling initiative not only reinforces the brand's mission but also encourages active participation and engagement from its audience.

By consistently telling its "One for One" story across multiple touchpoints and encouraging customer participation, TOMS has created a strong, emotionally resonant brand identity that sets it apart from competitors and inspires customer loyalty and advocacy.

Airbnb

Airbnb, the online marketplace for unique accommodations and experiences, has effectively used storytelling to build its brand identity and connect with its audience. The brand's storytelling focuses on the themes of belonging, community, and the transformative power of travel.

Airbnb's origin story is a compelling narrative that highlights the brand's humble beginnings and its founders' vision. The story goes that in 2007, roommates Brian Chesky and Joe Gebbia couldn't afford to pay their rent in San Francisco. They noticed that all the hotels in the city were booked due to a design conference, so they decided to rent out air mattresses in their living room and provide breakfast for their guests. This experience sparked the idea for Airbnb, a platform that would allow people to rent out their extra space to travellers looking for unique, authentic accommodations.

This origin story not only showcases the brand's innovative and entrepreneurial spirit but also sets the stage for its core mission of creating a world where anyone can belong anywhere. Airbnb consistently reinforces this message of belonging across its various touchpoints, from its website and social media to its advertising campaigns.

One of the most powerful ways Airbnb uses storytelling is through its user stories. The brand's "Stories from the Airbnb Community" series features real hosts and guests from around the world sharing their unique experiences and connections made through the platform. These stories range from heartwarming tales of cross-cultural friendships to inspiring accounts of personal growth and discovery.

By showcasing these user stories, Airbnb indirectly highlights the benefits of its platform, such as fostering meaningful connections, enabling unique travel experiences, and empowering individuals to be hosts and entrepreneurs. These stories create an emotional connection with the audience and help to differentiate Airbnb from traditional travel brands.

Airbnb's "Live There" campaign is another example of how the brand uses storytelling to emphasize user empowerment and transformation. The campaign features a series of short films that showcase the authentic, immersive experiences of travelers who "live like locals" in Airbnb accommodations. These stories focus on the personal growth, cultural enrichment, and sense of belonging that come from truly experiencing a destination rather than simply visiting as a tourist.

Through these user stories, Airbnb subtly communicates the benefits of its platform without directly promoting its product features. The brand's storytelling puts the spotlight on its community of hosts and guests, emphasizing the human connections and transformative experiences made possible by Airbnb.

In addition to its advertising campaigns, Airbnb incorporates storytelling into its website and booking experience. Each accommodation listing features a host profile with a personal story and photos, helping to create a sense of connection and trust between hosts and guests. The brand also encourages guests to share their own stories and experiences through reviews and social media, further amplifying the sense of community and belonging.

By consistently telling stories that showcase its community, values, and the transformative power of travel, Airbnb has built a strong, differentiated brand identity that resonates with its target audience. The brand's storytelling approach has helped it to stand out in the competitive travel industry and foster a deep sense of loyalty and advocacy among its users.

In conclusion, the Law of Storytelling highlights the importance of using narrative to create meaningful, memorable, and emotionally resonant connections with audiences. By crafting and sharing authentic, compelling stories that reflect their unique identity, values, and purpose, brands can differentiate themselves, build trust and credibility, and foster a sense of community and advocacy among their target audience.

* * *

13

The Law of Visual Design

In the world of branding, the Law of Visual Design emphasizes the crucial role that visual elements play in creating a strong, memorable, and effective brand identity. This law asserts that a brand's visual design should be distinctive, consistent, and aligned with its personality, values, and target audience.

Visual design encompasses all the graphical elements that make up a brand's identity, including its logo, color palette, typography, imagery, and overall aesthetic style. These elements work together to create a cohesive and recognizable visual language that communicates the brand's essence and sets it apart from competitors.

Here are some key reasons why visual design is essential for building a strong brand:

1. **First impressions:** Visual design is often the first point of contact between a brand and its audience. A well-designed logo, website, or product packaging can create a positive first impression and encourage further engagement with the brand.
2. **Brand recognition:** Consistent visual design helps to make a brand more recognizable and memorable. When a brand's visual elements are used consistently across various touchpoints, they become more easily

associated with the brand in the minds of consumers.
3. **Differentiation:** A distinctive visual design can help a brand stand out in a crowded market. By developing a unique visual language, a brand can differentiate itself from competitors and capture the attention of its target audience.
4. **Communication of brand personality:** Visual design elements can communicate a brand's personality, values, and tone of voice. For example, a brand targeting a younger, trendy audience might use bold colors and modern typography, while a brand emphasizing tradition and luxury might opt for a more classic, refined aesthetic.
5. **Emotional connection:** Effective visual design can evoke emotions and create a deeper connection between a brand and its audience. The right combination of colors, images, and design elements can inspire feelings of trust, excitement, or nostalgia, depending on the brand's goals.

To create a strong visual design that effectively represents your brand, consider the following tips:

1. **Develop a clear brand identity:** Before creating visual elements, define your brand's personality, values, and unique selling proposition. These foundational elements should guide your visual design choices.
2. **Ensure consistency:** Establish a set of visual guidelines that outline how your brand's visual elements should be used consistently across all touchpoints. This includes rules for logo usage, color palettes, typography, and imagery.
3. **Keep it simple:** A simple, uncluttered design is often more effective than a busy, complex one. Focus on creating visual elements that are easy to recognize and remember, even at a glance.
4. **Consider your target audience:** Your visual design should resonate with your target audience. Consider their preferences, values, and aesthetic sensibilities when making design choices.
5. **Invest in professional design:** Collaborate with experienced designers who can translate your brand identity into compelling visual elements.

High-quality, professional design can make a significant difference in how your brand is perceived.
6. **Adapt to different contexts:** While maintaining consistency, ensure that your visual design can adapt to different contexts and mediums, such as print, digital, and social media. This may require creating variations of your visual elements optimized for different platforms.

Apple

Apple's visual design is a masterclass in simplicity and minimalism. The company's iconic logo, an apple with a bite taken out of it, is one of the most recognizable logos in the world. The logo's sleek, simple design perfectly encapsulates Apple's brand identity, which is centred around innovation, user-friendliness, and elegant design.

Apple's product design is characterized by clean lines, smooth surfaces, and a focus on functionality. The company's products, from the iPhone to the MacBook, feature a minimalist aesthetic with a limited colour palette, usually consisting of white, black, and silver. This simple, uncluttered design language has become synonymous with Apple's brand and has influenced countless other technology companies.

In Apple's advertising and marketing materials, the focus is always on the product itself. The company often uses stark, white backgrounds to showcase its products, allowing the design of the devices to speak for itself. This approach reinforces the idea that Apple's products are the star of the show and that their design is a key selling point.

Apple's retail stores also reflect the company's minimalist visual design language. The stores feature open, uncluttered spaces with simple, clean lines and a focus on product displays. The use of glass, wood, and stainless steel creates a sense of sophistication and modernity, while the minimalist layout allows customers to easily interact with Apple's products.

Coca-Cola

Coca-Cola's visual identity is one of the most iconic and enduring in the world. The company's distinctive red and white colour scheme, cursive logo, and classic bottle shape have remained largely unchanged for over a century, making Coca-Cola instantly recognizable to consumers around the globe.

The Coca-Cola logo, with its cursive script and swooping "C," is a masterpiece of typography. The logo's design conveys a sense of fun, excitement, and nostalgia, perfectly capturing the brand's personality. The red and white colour scheme, which has been associated with Coca-Cola since the late 1800s, is bold, eye-catching, and has become synonymous with the brand.

Coca-Cola's classic glass bottle, with its curved shape and distinctive ribbing, is another key element of the brand's visual identity. The bottle's design, which was inspired by the shape of a cocoa bean, has become an icon in its own right and has been celebrated in art, music, and popular culture.

In its advertising and marketing campaigns, Coca-Cola often leverages its iconic visual elements to create a sense of nostalgia, happiness, and togetherness. The company's ads frequently feature people of diverse backgrounds coming together to enjoy a Coke, reinforcing the brand's message of unity and positivity.

Coca-Cola's visual design is also consistently applied across all touchpoints, from product packaging and point-of-sale materials to digital media and experiential marketing. This consistency helps to reinforce the brand's identity and make it instantly recognizable to consumers.

Chanel

Chanel's visual design is the epitome of luxury, sophistication, and timeless elegance. The fashion house's iconic interlocking C logo, which was designed by founder Coco Chanel herself, has become a symbol of high fashion and is instantly recognizable around the world.

Chanel's visual identity is characterized by a simple, monochromatic colour palette of black and white, with occasional pops of gold or red. This colour scheme communicates a sense of refinement, elegance, and exclusivity, perfectly aligning with the brand's luxury positioning.

In its product design, Chanel is known for its classic, timeless pieces that never go out of style. From the iconic Chanel No. 5 perfume bottle to the brand's signature tweed jackets and quilted handbags, Chanel's products feature clean lines, simple shapes, and exquisite attention to detail. This design language reflects the brand's commitment to quality, craftsmanship, and enduring style.

Chanel's packaging design is equally sophisticated and elegant. The brand's products are often packaged in sleek, black boxes with white lettering, creating a sense of anticipation and exclusivity. The use of high-quality materials, such as textured paper and satin ribbons, adds to the luxurious experience of unboxing a Chanel product.

In its advertising campaigns, Chanel often features black-and-white photography, evoking a sense of timeless glamour and sophistication. The brand frequently collaborates with high-profile celebrities and models, further reinforcing its status as a luxury fashion leader.

Chanel's visual design is consistently applied across all touchpoints, from its boutiques and product packaging to its digital presence and advertising campaigns. This consistency helps to reinforce the brand's identity and create a cohesive, luxurious experience for customers.

These three brands demonstrate the power of strong, consistent visual design in building a recognizable, memorable, and effective brand identity. By leveraging distinctive colour palettes, iconic logos, and consistent design languages, Apple, Coca-Cola, and Chanel have created visual identities that are instantly recognizable and deeply ingrained in popular culture. Their success underscores the importance of investing in high-quality, strategic visual design that aligns with a brand's personality, values, and target audience.

In conclusion, the Law of Visual Design underscores the importance of creating a distinctive, consistent, and emotionally resonant visual identity for your brand. By investing in high-quality, strategic visual design, you can differentiate your brand, communicate its personality, and create a lasting connection with your target audience.

* * *

14

The Law of Consistency

The Law of Consistency is a crucial principle in branding that emphasizes the importance of maintaining a cohesive and unified brand identity across all touchpoints and interactions with customers. Consistency in branding helps to build trust, credibility, and recognition among your target audience.

Consistent branding involves ensuring that all elements of your brand, including visual design, messaging, tone of voice, and customer experience, align with your brand's core values, purpose, and personality. By presenting a consistent brand identity, you create a strong and memorable impression in the minds of your customers, making it easier for them to recognize and connect with your brand.

Here are some key aspects of the Law of Consistency:

1. **Visual consistency:** Ensure that your brand's visual elements, such as logo, color palette, typography, and imagery, are used consistently across all marketing materials, products, and platforms. This helps to create a strong visual identity that is easily recognizable and memorable.
2. **Messaging consistency:** Your brand's messaging should be consistent in terms of tone, voice, and key messages. This includes your brand's tagline, mission statement, product descriptions, and marketing copy.

Consistent messaging reinforces your brand's values and helps to build a clear and compelling brand narrative.
3. **Customer experience consistency:** Deliver a consistent customer experience across all touchpoints, including your website, social media, customer service, and in-store interactions. This helps to build trust and loyalty among your customers, as they know what to expect from your brand regardless of how they engage with it.
4. **Consistency over time:** Maintain consistency in your branding efforts over time, even as your business grows and evolves. While it's important to adapt to changing market conditions and customer needs, your brand's core identity should remain stable and recognizable.
5. **Internal consistency:** Ensure that your employees understand and embody your brand's values, purpose, and personality. Consistent internal branding helps to create a strong company culture and ensures that your employees deliver a consistent brand experience to customers.

By adhering to the Law of Consistency, you can build a strong, memorable, and trustworthy brand that resonates with your target audience. Consistency in branding helps to differentiate your brand from competitors, build brand equity, and foster long-term customer loyalty.

Coca-Cola

Coca-Cola is a prime example of a brand that has maintained consistency over its long history. The company's iconic logo, featuring the distinctive red and white color scheme and the classic Spencerian script, has remained largely unchanged since its creation in the late 1800s. This visual consistency has helped to make Coca-Cola one of the most recognizable brands in the world.

In addition to its visual identity, Coca-Cola has maintained consistency in its messaging and brand personality. The brand is known for its upbeat, optimistic, and inclusive tone, often focusing on themes of happiness, togetherness, and celebration. This consistent messaging is evident in the company's advertising campaigns, such as "Share a Coke" and "Open Happiness," which reinforce the brand's core values and emotional appeal.

Coca-Cola also ensures consistency in its product offerings, with a focus on delivering a consistent taste and quality across its beverage portfolio. The company has been careful to maintain the secret formula of its flagship product, Coca-Cola, ensuring that customers can expect the same taste experience regardless of where they purchase the product.

Apple

Apple is another brand that exemplifies the Law of Consistency. The company has built a strong and recognizable brand identity through its consistent use of minimalist design, clean lines, and a focus on user experience. Apple's products, from the iPhone to the MacBook, feature a distinctive design language that is instantly recognizable and associated with the brand.

Apple's consistency extends beyond its visual identity to its messaging and brand personality. The company is known for its innovative, creative, and premium positioning, with a focus on empowering individuals through technology. This messaging is consistently communicated through Apple's advertising campaigns, product launches, and customer interactions.

In terms of customer experience, Apple ensures consistency through its retail stores, which feature a distinctive layout, design, and customer service approach. The Apple Store experience is designed to be consistent worldwide, with knowledgeable staff, hands-on product demonstrations, and a focus on customer education and support.

Apple also maintains consistency in its product ecosystem, ensuring that its devices and services work seamlessly together. This consistency creates a cohesive and integrated user experience, reinforcing the brand's commitment to simplicity and ease of use.

By consistently delivering on its brand promise and maintaining a cohesive brand identity across all touchpoints, Apple has built a loyal and dedicated customer base and established itself as a leader in the technology industry.

In conclusion, the Law of Consistency is a critical principle in branding that emphasizes the importance of maintaining a cohesive and unified brand identity across all touchpoints and interactions with customers. By consistently delivering on your brand promise and maintaining a strong visual, messaging, and experiential identity, you can build trust, credibility, and loyalty among your target audience. However, it's important to note that consistency doesn't mean rigidity. As your brand grows and evolves, there may be instances where you need to adapt your branding to stay relevant and connected with your audience. The key is to maintain the core essence of your brand while making strategic adjustments to stay current and engaging.

* * *

15

The Law of Archetypes

In the world of branding, the Law of Archetypes suggests that brands can create a deeper and more meaningful connection with their target audience by embodying a specific archetype. Archetypes are universal patterns of behavior, symbolism, and storytelling that have been present in human culture for centuries. By aligning with an archetype, brands can tap into the collective unconscious of their audience and create a strong emotional resonance.

The concept of archetypes was popularized by psychologist Carl Jung, who identified 12 primary archetypes that represent fundamental human motivations and desires. These archetypes include the Innocent, the Explorer, the Sage, the Hero, the Outlaw, the Magician, the Regular Guy/Girl, the Lover, the Jester, the Caregiver, the Creator, and the Ruler.

Here are some key aspects of the Law of Archetypes in branding:

1. **Identify your brand archetype:** The first step in applying the Law of Archetypes is to identify which archetype best aligns with your brand's values, personality, and mission. This requires a deep understanding of your brand's core essence and the needs and desires of your target audience.
2. **Embody the archetype:** Once you have identified your brand archetype,

the next step is to consistently embody that archetype across all aspects of your brand experience. This includes your visual identity, messaging, storytelling, customer experience, and product design.
3. **Create a narrative:** Archetypes are often associated with specific narratives and storylines. By creating a compelling brand narrative that aligns with your chosen archetype, you can create a deeper emotional connection with your audience and differentiate your brand from competitors.
4. **Evoke emotion:** Archetypes are powerful because they tap into deep-seated human emotions and desires. By embodying an archetype, brands can evoke strong emotional responses in their audience, such as inspiration, empowerment, or belonging.
5. **Maintain consistency:** To effectively leverage the power of archetypes, brands must maintain consistency in their archetype expression across all touchpoints. Inconsistency can undermine the authenticity and credibility of the brand's archetype alignment.
6. **Evolve with your audience:** As your brand and audience evolve over time, it may be necessary to adjust your archetype alignment to remain relevant and resonant. This requires ongoing research and analysis to understand shifts in audience needs and preferences.

By leveraging the Law of Archetypes, brands can create a deeper and more meaningful connection with their audience that goes beyond functional benefits and features. Archetypes provide a powerful framework for creating a cohesive and emotionally resonant brand experience that can differentiate your brand and drive long-term loyalty.

However, it's important to note that not all brands fit neatly into a single archetype, and some may embody multiple archetypes or evolve over time. The key is to identify the archetype that best aligns with your brand's core essence and the needs of your target audience, and to consistently express that archetype across all touchpoints.

Nike

Nike is a brand that embodies the Hero archetype. The Hero is characterized by courage, determination, and the desire to prove oneself through difficult challenges and obstacles. Nike's slogan, "Just Do It," perfectly encapsulates the Hero's spirit of resilience and perseverance in the face of adversity.

Nike's visual identity is also strongly aligned with the Hero archetype. The brand's iconic "swoosh" logo is a simple, yet powerful symbol that represents speed, motion, and forward progress. Nike's advertising and marketing often feature heroic imagery of athletes pushing themselves to the limit and overcoming challenges, reinforcing the brand's alignment with the Hero archetype.

Nike's brand narrative is also deeply rooted in the Hero's journey. Many of the brand's most iconic campaigns, such as "Find Your Greatness" and "Dream Crazy," feature stories of athletes who have overcome significant obstacles and achieved greatness through sheer determination and hard work. These stories are designed to inspire and empower Nike's audience, evoking strong emotions of pride, determination, and self-belief.

Nike's product design also reflects the Hero archetype, with a focus on performance, innovation, and pushing the boundaries of what's possible. Nike's products are designed to help athletes achieve their goals and reach their full potential, whether it's through advanced technology, innovative materials, or customized design.

Throughout its history, Nike has consistently embodied the Hero archetype across all touchpoints, from advertising and marketing to product design and customer experience. This consistency has helped to create a strong and authentic brand identity that resonates with Nike's target audience of athletes and fitness enthusiasts.

However, Nike has also demonstrated the ability to evolve and adapt its archetype expression over time. In recent years, the brand has placed a greater emphasis on social and political activism, taking a stand on issues such as racial justice and gender equality. This evolution reflects a broader shift in the needs and values of Nike's audience, and demonstrates the brand's ability to adapt its archetype alignment to remain relevant and resonant.

Nike has also leveraged the power of storytelling to create a deep emotional connection with its audience. The brand's "Dream Crazy" campaign, featuring former NFL quarterback Colin Kaepernick, is a powerful example of how Nike uses storytelling to evoke strong emotions and inspire its audience to pursue their dreams and fight for what they believe in.

Overall, Nike's successful leveraging of the Hero archetype demonstrates the power of the Law of Archetypes in creating strong and resonant brands. By consistently embodying the Hero's values of courage, determination, and perseverance, and by using storytelling to create deep emotional connections with its audience, Nike has built one of the most iconic and successful brands in the world.

Apple

Another excellent example of a brand that effectively leverages the Law of Archetypes is Apple, which embodies the Creator archetype.

The Creator archetype is characterized by a desire for innovation, self-expression, and the creation of something new and valuable. Apple's mission statement, "to bring the best user experience to its customers through its innovative hardware, software, and services," perfectly aligns with the Creator archetype's values.

Apple's visual identity is sleek, minimalist, and highly distinctive, reflecting the Creator's focus on simplicity, elegance, and innovation. The brand's iconic logo, a simple apple with a bite taken out of it, is a powerful symbol of knowledge, creativity, and thinking differently.

Apple's brand narrative is centered around the idea of empowering individuals to create and express themselves through technology. The brand's advertising and marketing often feature stories of creators, artists, and innovators who use Apple products to bring their ideas to life and make a positive impact on the world.

Apple's product design is also strongly aligned with the Creator archetype, with a focus on intuitive, user-friendly interfaces, high-quality materials, and cutting-edge technology. Apple's products are designed to inspire creativity and enable users to express themselves in new and innovative ways, whether it's through music, photography, video, or graphic design.

Throughout its history, Apple has consistently embodied the Creator archetype across all touchpoints, from its iconic advertising campaigns like "Think Different" to its sleek and minimalist retail stores. This consistency has helped to create a strong and authentic brand identity that resonates with Apple's target audience of creatives, innovators, and tech enthusiasts.

However, like Nike, Apple has also demonstrated the ability to evolve and adapt its archetype expression over time. In recent years, the brand has placed a greater emphasis on privacy, security, and social responsibility, reflecting a broader shift in the needs and values of its audience.

Apple has also leveraged the power of storytelling to create a deep emotional connection with its audience. The brand's "Shot on iPhone" campaign, which features stunning photos and videos captured by iPhone users around the world, is a powerful example of how Apple uses storytelling to showcase the creativity and capabilities of its products.

Apple's successful leveraging of the Creator archetype demonstrates the power of the Law of Archetypes in creating strong and resonant brands.

In conclusion, the Law of Archetypes is a powerful principle for creating strong and resonant brands that connect with audiences on a deep emotional level. By embodying a specific archetype and creating a cohesive and authentic brand experience, brands can differentiate themselves, evoke strong emotions, and build lasting relationships with their customers. As the marketplace becomes increasingly crowded and competitive, the Law of Archetypes provides a valuable framework for creating brands that stand out and inspire loyal followings.

* * *

16

The Law of Timing

In the fast-paced and ever-changing world of branding, the Law of Timing emphasizes the critical importance of launching and executing brand strategies at the right moment for maximum impact and success. Timing can make or break a brand's efforts to capture attention, resonate with audiences, and establish a strong market presence.

The Law of Timing involves a deep understanding of market trends, consumer behaviour, and cultural zeitgeist. Brands that are able to anticipate and capitalize on emerging opportunities, while also being agile enough to adapt to unexpected challenges, are better positioned to succeed in the long run.

Here are some key aspects of the Law of Timing in branding:

1. **Monitor market trends:** Brands must continuously monitor market trends and consumer behaviour to identify opportunities and anticipate shifts in demand. This involves staying up-to-date on industry news, conducting market research, and engaging with customers to understand their evolving needs and preferences.
2. **Anticipate cultural moments:** Successful brands are often those that are able to tap into cultural moments and align their messaging and offerings with the zeitgeist. This requires a deep understanding of

popular culture, social issues, and consumer values, as well as the ability to anticipate and respond to cultural shifts in real time.
3. **Embrace agility:** In today's fast-paced and unpredictable business environment, brands must be agile and adaptable to succeed. This means being able to quickly pivot strategies, messaging, and offerings in response to changing market conditions, consumer feedback, or unexpected events.
4. **Capitalize on innovation:** Brands that are able to bring innovative products, services, or experiences to market at the right time can capture a significant competitive advantage. This requires a combination of creativity, market insight, and the ability to execute quickly and effectively.
5. **Balance proactivity and reactivity:** Successful brands strike a balance between being proactive in anticipating and shaping market trends and being reactive in responding to unexpected challenges or opportunities. This requires a combination of long-term strategic planning and short-term tactical agility.
6. **Consider seasonality:** Many industries are influenced by seasonal factors, such as holidays, weather patterns, or cultural events. Brands that are able to effectively plan and execute seasonal campaigns and offerings can capitalize on peak demand periods and build strong associations with specific times of the year.

By leveraging the Law of Timing, brands can create a strong and enduring market presence that resonates with audiences and drives long-term growth. However, the Law of Timing also requires brands to be constantly vigilant and adaptable, as the window of opportunity for any given strategy or initiative can be fleeting.

Successful brands are those that are able to anticipate and capitalize on emerging opportunities while also being agile enough to pivot quickly in response to unexpected challenges or shifts in the market. This requires a combination of deep market insight, creative thinking, and execution excellence.

OREO

One of the most famous examples of Oreo's mastery of timing occurred during the 2013 Super Bowl, when a power outage caused a unexpected 34-minute delay in the game. Within minutes of the blackout, Oreo's social media team tweeted an ad featuring an image of a single Oreo cookie in the spotlight with the caption, "You can still dunk in the dark." The tweet quickly went viral, generating thousands of retweets and likes, and earning Oreo widespread praise for its quick thinking and creativity.

Oreo's Super Bowl tweet is a perfect example of how brands can capitalize on unexpected cultural moments to create a strong and memorable impression on audiences. By being agile and responsive in real-time, Oreo was able to turn a potentially negative situation into a positive brand-building opportunity.

But Oreo's success with timing goes beyond just one tweet. The brand has a long history of leveraging seasonal and cultural moments to create timely and relevant marketing campaigns. For example, Oreo regularly releases limited-edition flavors tied to holidays and special events, such as Peppermint Bark Oreos for the winter holidays or Peeps Oreos for Easter.

Oreo has also been effective at tapping into broader cultural trends and movements. In 2012, the brand released a rainbow-colored "Pride" cookie as a show of support for the LGBTQ+ community. The move generated significant buzz and goodwill for the brand, while also positioning Oreo as a socially conscious and inclusive company.

In addition to its cultural relevance, Oreo has also been effective at anticipating and shaping market trends. In recent years, the brand has expanded beyond its classic cookie offerings to include new product lines such as Oreo Thins and Oreo Minis, which cater to changing consumer preferences for snacking and portion control.

Oreo's success with the Law of Timing can be attributed to several key factors. First, the brand has a deep understanding of its target audience and what resonates with them culturally and emotionally. Second, Oreo has built a strong and adaptable brand identity that allows it to be flexible and responsive to changing market conditions. Finally, the brand has invested in the capabilities and resources needed to execute quickly and effectively in real-time, whether it's through social media, product innovation, or marketing campaigns.

By anticipating and capitalizing on emerging opportunities while also being adaptable enough to pivot quickly when needed, Oreo has built a strong and enduring brand that continues to resonate with audiences around the world.

Nike Presto

In the 1980s, Nike was the dominant player in the athletic footwear market, commanding a majority of the market share. However, the brand recognized that its dominance in the performance market left little room for further growth. To continue expanding, Nike needed to identify new opportunities and anticipate emerging trends.

Nike's team focused on understanding the "next generation of young athletes" and the cultural movements that would shape their preferences and behaviours. Through continuous observation and market research, Nike's designers noticed a curious phenomenon in the fashion world at the time: the dominance of black. From window displays to suits and accessories, black was everywhere, creating a sombre and monochromatic aesthetic.

Anticipating Cultural Shifts: Nike's team astutely interpreted this "black phenomenon" as a sign that people would soon become interested in brighter, bolder colors again. They anticipated that consumers would seek ways to add pops of colour to their all-black outfits, creating a new opportunity for athletic footwear that could serve as a vibrant accessory.

Capitalizing on Market Opportunities: Armed with this insight, Nike's designers set out to create a shoe that would capitalize on the impending shift towards brighter colours. They developed the Nike Presto, a shoe featuring eight individual colours, including eye-catching shades of red, orange, and green. This bold and unconventional design was a departure from Nike's typical aesthetic, but the brand was willing to take a calculated risk to seize the emerging opportunity.

Executing Quickly and Effectively: Once the Presto concept was finalized, Nike moved swiftly to bring the product to market. The brand leveraged its extensive manufacturing and distribution capabilities to ensure that the Presto would be available to consumers as soon as the trend towards brighter colours began to take hold. This quick and effective execution allowed Nike to capitalize on the opportunity before competitors could respond.

The Overnight Sensation: When the Nike Presto launched, it was an immediate sensation. Consumers eagerly embraced the shoe's vibrant colours and unique design, seeing it as a fresh and exciting addition to their wardrobes. The Presto became a must-have item, generating significant buzz and sales for Nike.

The success of the Nike Presto demonstrates the power of the Law of Timing in branding. By anticipating cultural shifts, identifying untapped market opportunities, taking calculated risks, and executing quickly and effectively, Nike was able to create a product that perfectly captured the zeitgeist of the moment. The Presto not only resonated with consumers' evolving tastes but also helped to establish Nike as a leader in the athletic footwear market and a brand that was attuned to the pulse of popular culture.

Maclaren's BMW Buggy Baby Stroller

Maclaren, a renowned British company known for its high-quality baby strollers, demonstrated a keen understanding of the Law of Timing when it recognized a significant shift in parental roles and its potential impact on the baby products market.

Observing Cultural Shifts: Through market research and observing cultural trends, Maclaren noticed that more men were taking on the role of primary caregivers for their newborn babies. This shift in parental responsibilities meant that men were becoming increasingly involved in purchasing decisions for baby products, a domain traditionally controlled by women.

Identifying Untapped Opportunities: Recognizing this changing dynamic,

Maclaren saw an untapped opportunity to cater to the preferences and needs of this growing segment of male caregivers. The company understood that to capitalize on this trend, it needed to create a product that would appeal specifically to men, breaking away from the conventional designs and marketing approaches in the baby stroller market.

Taking a Bold Approach: Maclaren took a bold and innovative approach to seize this opportunity by partnering with BMW, the iconic German car manufacturer known for its sleek design and high-performance engineering. Together, they developed the BMW Buggy Baby Stroller, a product that combined Maclaren's expertise in baby strollers with BMW's signature style and technical prowess.

Designing for a New Audience: The BMW Buggy Baby Stroller was designed with a focus on the preferences and needs of modern fathers. The stroller featured a sleek, sporty design reminiscent of BMW's luxury cars, with a black and silver colour scheme, clean lines, and premium materials. It also incorporated advanced features such as a suspension system for a smooth ride and a lightweight, compact folding mechanism for easy storage and transport.

Launching at the Right Moment: Maclaren strategically launched the BMW Buggy Baby Stroller at a time when the trend of fathers as primary caregivers was gaining significant momentum. By introducing the product at the right moment, Maclaren was able to capture the attention of its target audience and establish itself as a brand that understood and catered to the evolving needs of modern parents.

This example demonstrates how brands can leverage the Law of Timing by staying attuned to cultural movements, anticipating changing consumer needs and taking calculated risks to introducing products that align with emerging trends.

In conclusion, the Law of Timing is a critical principle for building strong and successful brands in today's fast-paced and ever-changing business environment. By monitoring market trends, anticipating cultural moments, embracing agility, and balancing proactivity and reactivity, brands can create a strong and enduring market presence that resonates with audiences and drives long-term growth. As the pace of change continues to accelerate, the Law of Timing will only become more important for brands seeking to stay ahead of the curve and build lasting success in the marketplace.

* * *

IV

Part 04—Brand Experience

17

The Law of Experiential Branding

In today's competitive market, customers are seeking more than just products or services; they are looking for meaningful experiences that connect with them on an emotional level. The Law of Experiential Branding emphasizes the importance of creating memorable, engaging, and immersive brand experiences that leave a lasting impression on customers.

Experiential branding goes beyond traditional marketing tactics, focusing on creating multi-sensory experiences that engage customers and foster a deeper connection with the brand. By creating experiences that are authentic, relevant, and valuable to customers, brands can differentiate themselves from competitors and build lasting loyalty.

Here are some key aspects of the Law of Experiential Branding:

1. **Engage multiple senses:** Create experiences that engage multiple senses, such as sight, sound, touch, taste, and smell. Multi-sensory experiences are more memorable and can help to create a stronger emotional connection with customers.
2. **Create immersive environments:** Design immersive brand environments that transport customers into the world of your brand. This can include branded retail spaces, pop-up experiences, or interactive installations that allow customers to fully engage with your brand.
3. **Offer personalized experiences:** Tailor experiences to individual cus-

tomers based on their preferences, needs, and behaviours. Personalized experiences make customers feel valued and understood, fostering a stronger sense of brand loyalty.
4. **Leverage technology:** Incorporate technology, such as augmented reality, virtual reality, or interactive displays, to create innovative and engaging brand experiences. Technology can help to create a sense of wonder and excitement around your brand.
5. **Create shareable moments:** Design experiences that are shareable and invite customers to document and share their experiences on social media. Shareable moments can help amplify your brand's reach and generate buzz around your experiential campaigns.
6. **Align experiences with brand values:** Ensure that your experiential branding efforts align with your brand's core values, personality, and purpose. Authentic experiences that are true to your brand's identity are more likely to resonate with customers and build trust.

By embracing the Law of Experiential Branding, brands can create meaningful and memorable connections with customers that go beyond traditional marketing tactics. Experiential branding can help to differentiate your brand, build brand loyalty, and drive customer advocacy.

However, it's important to note that experiential branding requires a significant investment of time, resources, and creativity. Brands must carefully plan and execute their experiential campaigns to ensure that they are authentic, relevant, and valuable to customers. Additionally, brands must be prepared to measure the success of their experiential efforts and continuously iterate and improve based on customer feedback and insights.

Disney

Disney is a master of experiential branding, creating immersive and magical experiences that transport guests into the world of their favourite stories and characters. From the moment guests step into a Disney theme park, they are greeted with a meticulously designed environment that engages all five senses.

Disney's attention to detail is evident in every aspect of the guest experience, from the architecture and landscaping to the music and character interactions. The company's theme parks feature iconic attractions, such as Pirates of the Caribbean and It's a Small World, that immerse guests in rich storytelling and create lasting memories.

Disney also extends its experiential branding beyond its theme parks, with initiatives such as the Disney Cruise Line and Disney Stores. These experiences are carefully crafted to align with Disney's brand values of magic, imagination, and storytelling, creating a consistent and cohesive brand experience across all touchpoints.

To personalize the guest experience, Disney offers tools such as the My Disney Experience app, which allows guests to plan their visit, make dining reservations, and access real-time wait times for attractions. Disney also offers personalized experiences, such as the Bibbidi Bobbidi Boutique, where children can be transformed into their favourite princess or knight.

IKEA

IKEA, the Swedish furniture retailer, has built a strong brand through its unique and immersive in-store experiences. IKEA's stores are designed to be a destination in themselves, offering a full day of shopping, dining, and entertainment.

Upon entering an IKEA store, customers are guided through a carefully designed showroom that showcases the company's products in realistic and inspiring room settings. Customers can touch and interact with the products, envisioning how they might fit into their own homes. The showroom experience is designed to be self-guided, allowing customers to explore at their own pace and discover new ideas and inspiration.

IKEA also offers a range of in-store experiences that extend beyond shopping, such as the IKEA Restaurant, which serves Swedish meatballs and other Scandinavian cuisine. The restaurant provides a welcome break from shopping and allows customers to immerse themselves in Swedish culture and cuisine.

To personalize the customer experience, IKEA offers a range of planning tools and services, such as the IKEA Home Planner, which allows customers to design and visualize their dream kitchen or wardrobe. IKEA also offers in-store consultations with design experts who can provide personalized advice and recommendations.

IKEA's experiential branding efforts are designed to create a sense of community and belonging among its customers. The company regularly hosts in-store events and workshops, such as cooking classes and DIY tutorials, that bring customers together and foster a sense of connection with the brand.

In both of these examples, Disney and IKEA have created immersive and engaging brand experiences that go beyond traditional marketing tactics. By offering personalized, multi-sensory experiences that align with their brand values and personality, these companies have built strong emotional connections with their customers and created a competitive advantage in their respective industries. Through their experiential branding efforts, Disney and IKEA have set a high bar for other brands looking to create memorable and meaningful customer experiences.

In conclusion, the Law of Experiential Branding is a powerful principle that emphasizes the importance of creating memorable, engaging, and immersive brand experiences that connect with customers on an emotional level. By offering personalized, multi-sensory experiences that align with your brand's values and personality, you can differentiate your brand, build lasting loyalty, and create a competitive advantage in today's crowded market. As customers increasingly seek out experiences over products, brands that embrace experiential branding will be well-positioned for success in the years to come.

* * *

18

The Law of Holistic Experience Design

In today's competitive market, creating a strong and memorable brand requires more than just delivering great products or services. The Law of Holistic Experience Design emphasizes the importance of crafting seamless, engaging, and consistent experiences across all customer touchpoints, from initial awareness to post-purchase support.

Holistic experience design recognizes that every interaction a customer has with your brand, whether online or offline, contributes to their overall perception and relationship with your brand. By intentionally designing and orchestrating these touchpoints to create a cohesive and compelling brand experience, you can build stronger emotional connections, increase customer loyalty, and differentiate your brand from competitors.

Here are some key aspects of the Law of Holistic Experience Design:

1. **Map the customer journey:** Identify all the touchpoints where customers interact with your brand, including your website, social media, advertising, in-store experiences, customer service, and post-purchase support. Map out the customer journey to understand how customers move through these touchpoints and identify opportunities to enhance the experience.
2. **Ensure consistency:** Maintain a consistent brand identity, messaging,

and tone across all touchpoints. Consistency helps to build trust and credibility with customers and reinforces your brand's unique personality and values.
3. **Optimize for each touchpoint:** While maintaining consistency, tailor the experience to the specific context and needs of each touchpoint. For example, the experience on your mobile app should be optimized for the unique constraints and opportunities of mobile devices, while your in-store experience should focus on creating an immersive and engaging environment.
4. **Personalize the experience:** Use data and customer insights to personalize the experience at each touchpoint. Personalization can include tailored product recommendations, customized content, or personalized service based on the customer's preferences and behaviors.
5. **Engage the senses:** Create multi-sensory experiences that engage customers on an emotional level. Incorporate elements such as visual design, sound, scent, and texture to create a more immersive and memorable experience.
6. **Continuously measure and improve:** Regularly gather customer feedback and data to measure the effectiveness of your holistic experience design. Use these insights to continuously refine and improve the experience, identifying areas for optimization and innovation.

By embracing the Law of Holistic Experience Design, brands can create a competitive advantage by delivering exceptional experiences that engage customers on a deeper level. When customers have a positive and memorable experience with your brand across all touchpoints, they are more likely to become loyal advocates who recommend your brand to others.

However, implementing a holistic experience design requires a significant investment of time, resources, and cross-functional collaboration. It requires a customer-centric mindset and a willingness to break down organizational silos to create a seamless and integrated experience. Brands must also be prepared to adapt and evolve their experience design over time, as customer needs and preferences change.

Starbucks

Starbucks is an excellent example of a brand that has successfully embraced the Law of Holistic Experience Design, creating a consistent and engaging experience across all customer touchpoints.

From the moment customers enter a Starbucks store, they are immersed in a carefully crafted environment that engages all five senses. The store design features warm colours, comfortable seating, and inviting lighting that creates a welcoming and relaxing atmosphere. The aroma of freshly brewed coffee and baked goods fills the air, enticing customers to stay and linger.

Starbucks also places a strong emphasis on personalization, with baristas trained to greet customers by name and remember their regular orders. The company's mobile app allows customers to order and pay ahead, customize their drinks, and earn rewards, creating a seamless and convenient experience.

Beyond the in-store experience, Starbucks has extended its holistic experience design to other touchpoints, such as its website, social media, and advertising. The company's website features a clean and intuitive design that showcases its products and values, with engaging content such as recipes and brewing tips. Starbucks' social media presence is highly interactive, with the brand regularly responding to customer inquiries and sharing user-generated content.

Starbucks also uses its advertising to reinforce its brand values and create an emotional connection with customers. The company's campaigns often focus on themes of community, connection, and social responsibility, such as its "Upstanders" series, which highlights inspiring stories of ordinary people making a difference in their communities.

To further enhance the customer experience, Starbucks has introduced a range of innovative initiatives and partnerships. For example, the company has partnered with Spotify to create a custom music playlist for each store, creating a unique and engaging audio experience. Starbucks has also introduced Reserve Roasteries, which offer an immersive and educational coffee experience, with expert baristas and interactive displays that showcase the coffee-making process.

Starbucks also places a strong emphasis on social responsibility and sustainability, which is integrated into all aspects of the customer experience. The company has committed to using ethically sourced coffee, reducing waste, and supporting local communities, which resonates with customers who value brands that make a positive impact.

To continuously measure and improve the customer experience, Starbucks regularly gathers feedback through surveys, focus groups, and social media listening. The company uses this data to identify areas for improvement and innovation, such as introducing new products or optimizing store layouts.

Overall, Starbucks has created a holistic experience design that is consistent, engaging, and emotionally resonant across all touchpoints. By paying attention to every detail of the customer journey, from the in-store environment to mobile ordering and social responsibility initiatives, Starbucks has built a loyal and passionate customer base that sees the brand as more than just a coffee company, but a valued part of their daily lives.

Apple iPod

The iPod is a great example of how Apple applied the Law of Holistic Experience Design to create a seamless and engaging experience around a specific product.

When Apple introduced the iPod in 2001, it revolutionized the way people listened to music on the go. The device itself featured a sleek and minimalist design, with a simple and intuitive user interface that made it easy to navigate and control. The click wheel became an iconic feature of the iPod, allowing users to quickly scroll through their music library and adjust volume and playback settings.

However, the iPod experience extended far beyond the device itself. Apple created a holistic ecosystem around the iPod that included hardware, software, and services, all designed to work together seamlessly.

On the software side, Apple introduced iTunes, a digital media player that allowed users to easily manage their music library, create playlists, and sync their content with their iPod. iTunes also served as a marketplace store where users could purchase and download music, making it easy to discover and acquire new content.

Apple also designed a range of accessories that enhanced the iPod experience, such as custom earbuds, docking stations, and cases. These accessories not only provided additional functionality but also reinforced the iPod's distinctive brand identity.

The iPod experience was also integrated into Apple's broader ecosystem of products and services. For example, users could easily connect their iPod to their Mac or PC to sync their music library, and later models of the iPod could also sync with Apple's cloud-based services like iCloud.

Apple's advertising and marketing for the iPod also played a key role in shaping the holistic experience. The company's iconic "silhouette" ads featured black silhouettes of people dancing against colourful backgrounds, with white iPod earbuds prominently displayed. These ads helped to establish the iPod as a cultural icon and reinforced the idea that the device was not just a music player but a lifestyle accessory.

To continuously improve the iPod experience, Apple gathered feedback from users through a variety of channels, including customer surveys, user testing, and data analytics. The company used this feedback to inform product development and introduce new features and improvements over time, such as larger storage capacities, color displays, and touch controls.

In conclusion, the Law of Holistic Experience Design is a powerful principle for building strong and memorable brands in today's experience-driven economy. By intentionally designing and orchestrating experiences across all customer touchpoints, brands can create deeper emotional connections, increase customer loyalty, and differentiate themselves from competitors. As customers increasingly seek out brands that deliver exceptional experiences, those that embrace holistic experience design will be well-positioned for success in the years to come.

THE TIMELESS LAWS OF BRANDING

* * *

19

The Law of Overdelivering

In the competitive world of branding, merely meeting customer expectations is no longer sufficient. To truly stand out and create lasting impressions, brands must go above and beyond at every customer touchpoint. The Law of Overdelivering states that brands should consistently exceed customer expectations, delivering exceptional value and experiences that surprise and delight. By making overdelivering a core principle of their brand strategy, companies can cultivate loyal customers, generate positive word-of-mouth, and establish a strong competitive advantage.

The Power of Exceeding Expectations

When brands overdeliver, they create memorable experiences that stick with customers long after the interaction has ended. The benefits of consistently exceeding expectations include:

1. Increased customer satisfaction and loyalty
2. Positive word-of-mouth and referrals
3. Differentiation from competitors
4. Enhanced perceived value of products or services
5. Improved brand reputation and equity

Strategies for Overdelivering at Customer Touchpoints

1. **Identify key touchpoints:** Map out the customer journey and identify the critical touchpoints where you have the opportunity to make a lasting impression. These touchpoints can include product quality, packaging, customer service, in-store experiences, website interactions, and post-purchase follow-up.
2. **Understand customer expectations:** Gather insights into what customers expect at each touchpoint through surveys, feedback, and market research. This understanding will serve as a baseline for identifying opportunities to overdeliver.
3. **Anticipate unstated needs:** Go beyond addressing customers' stated needs and anticipate their unstated or future needs. By proactively offering solutions or enhancements that customers haven't even considered, brands can demonstrate a deep understanding of their customers and create delightful surprises.
4. **Personalize the experience:** Use data and customer insights to personalize interactions and experiences. By tailoring offerings, communications, and experiences to individual preferences and needs, brands can make customers feel valued and appreciated, exceeding their expectations for personalized attention.
5. **Deliver exceptional service:** Train and empower employees to go above and beyond in delivering exceptional customer service. Encourage a culture of overdelivering, where employees are encouraged to find creative ways to surprise and delight customers at every interaction.
6. **Create memorable moments:** Look for opportunities to create memorable, shareable moments that exceed expectations. This can include unexpected gifts, personalized touches, or going out of the way to solve a customer's problem in a remarkable fashion.
7. **Continuously raise the bar:** As customer expectations evolve, brands must continuously raise the bar for overdelivering. Regularly assess and improve upon the ways in which you exceed expectations, staying ahead of the curve and setting new standards for customer experience.

Airbnb

Airbnb, the online marketplace for short-term rentals and experiences, has built its brand on the principle of overdelivering at each customer touchpoint. Co-founder Brian Chesky and his team have consistently pushed the boundaries of what it means to provide exceptional hospitality.

As Chesky explains, they start by imagining what a 5-star experience would look like at each touchpoint. For example, when a guest arrives at their rental, a 5-star experience might include a smooth check-in process and a clean, well-maintained space. But Chesky and his team don't stop there.

They then ask themselves, "What would a 6-star experience be?" This might include the host personally welcoming the guest, providing a thoughtful gift tailored to their interests, and stocking the fridge with water and the bathroom with high-quality toiletries.

But Airbnb takes it even further by envisioning a 7-star experience. This could involve the host going above and beyond by allowing the guest full use of the kitchen, organizing unique experiences like surfing lessons or restaurant reservations, or even providing a car for the guest to use during their stay.

By continually pushing the boundaries of what it means to overdeliver, Airbnb has created a brand that is synonymous with exceptional hospitality and unforgettable travel experiences. This approach has helped the company build a fiercely loyal customer base and differentiate itself in a crowded market.

The Ritz-Carlton

The Ritz-Carlton, a global luxury hotel chain, is renowned for its commitment to overdelivering at every customer touchpoint. The company's "Gold Standards" include a pledge to deliver the "ultimate guest experience," and employees are empowered to go above and beyond to fulfill this promise.

One of the most famous examples of The Ritz-Carlton's overdelivering culture involves a family staying at the Ritz-Carlton, Bali. The family's young son left his beloved stuffed giraffe, "Joshie," behind in the room when they checked out. When the family realized the toy was missing, they called the hotel, and the staff promised to find Joshie and send him home.

Not only did the hotel find Joshie, but they also created a memorable experience for the family. Before shipping the toy back, the staff took photos of Joshie enjoying various hotel amenities, such as getting a massage at the spa, lounging by the pool, and even "working" at the concierge desk. They compiled these photos into a booklet and sent it along with Joshie back to the family.

This act of overdelivering turned a potentially negative experience (losing a cherished toy) into a delightful, unforgettable moment for the family. It also reinforced The Ritz-Carlton's reputation for exceptional service and attention to detail.

The Ritz-Carlton empowers its employees to overdeliver by providing them with a budget of up to $2,000 per guest to resolve issues or create extraordinary experiences without needing management approval. This level of trust and autonomy allows staff to be creative and proactive in finding ways to exceed guest expectations.

By consistently overdelivering at every touchpoint, from check-in to room service to checkout, The Ritz-Carlton has built a brand that is synonymous with luxury, personalized service, and unforgettable experiences. This commitment to going above and beyond has helped the company cultivate a loyal customer base and maintain its position as a leader in the luxury hospitality industry.

In conclusion, by embracing the Law of Overdelivering, brands can create exceptional experiences that exceed customer expectations at every touchpoint. By consistently going above and beyond, brands can differentiate themselves, build loyal customer relationships, and establish a strong competitive advantage in the marketplace.

* * *

20

The Law of Consistency (Experience)

In the realm of branding, consistency is a fundamental principle that cannot be overlooked. The Law of Consistency (Experience) states that brands must deliver a consistent experience across all customer touchpoints, ensuring that every interaction reinforces the brand's core values, promises, and identity. By maintaining consistency, brands can build trust, familiarity, and loyalty among their customers, ultimately leading to a stronger, more resilient brand.

The Importance of Consistency in Brand Experience

Consistency in brand experience is crucial for several reasons:

1. **Builds trust:** When a brand consistently delivers on its promises and provides a reliable experience, customers learn to trust the brand and feel confident in their interactions with it.
2. **Creates familiarity:** Consistent experiences help customers become familiar with a brand, making it easier for them to recognize and remember the brand across various touchpoints.
3. **Reinforces brand identity:** By consistently communicating and embodying the brand's core values, personality, and unique selling proposition,

brands can strengthen their identity and differentiate themselves from competitors.
4. **Enhances customer loyalty:** Customers are more likely to remain loyal to a brand that consistently meets or exceeds their expectations, as they know what to expect and can rely on the brand to deliver.
5. **Increases brand equity:** Consistent, positive experiences contribute to a brand's overall reputation and value, driving increased brand equity over time.

Strategies for Maintaining Consistency in Brand Experience

1. **Define brand guidelines:** Establish clear brand guidelines that outline the brand's visual identity, messaging, tone of voice, and core values. These guidelines should be documented and shared with all stakeholders to ensure consistency across all touchpoints.
2. **Train employees:** Provide comprehensive training to all employees who interact with customers, ensuring they understand the brand's values, promises, and expected behaviours. Regularly reinforce this training to maintain consistency over time.
3. **Monitor and measure consistency:** Regularly assess the consistency of brand experiences across various touchpoints, using customer feedback, mystery shopping, and other evaluation methods. Identify areas for improvement and take corrective action as needed.
4. **Integrate systems and processes:** Ensure that all systems and processes, from customer service to product delivery, are designed to support and reinforce the desired brand experience. Consistency in operations is key to delivering a consistent customer experience.
5. **Adapt to customer needs:** While maintaining consistency, be flexible enough to adapt to individual customer needs and preferences. Strive to provide a consistent overall experience while tailoring interactions to each customer's unique situation.
6. **Continuously improve:** Regularly review and refine the brand experience based on customer feedback, market trends, and internal

assessments. Continuously seek ways to enhance consistency and improve the overall customer experience.

McDonald's

McDonald's, the global fast-food chain, is a prime example of a brand that has built its success on the Law of Consistency (Experience). With over 38,000 locations in more than 100 countries, McDonald's has managed to deliver a consistent experience to customers across the world.

One of the key elements of McDonald's consistency is its standardized menu. Customers can expect to find the same core menu items, such as Big Macs, Quarter Pounders, and French fries, in any McDonald's restaurant, regardless of location. This familiarity is comforting to customers and makes it easy for them to order their favorite meals without confusion.

McDonald's also maintains consistency in its restaurant design and layout. The company has established a recognizable aesthetic that includes bright colours, clean lines, and a welcoming atmosphere. This consistency extends to the drive-thru experience, where customers can expect a similar ordering process and wait times across locations.

In addition to its physical consistency, McDonald's has also invested heavily in training its employees to deliver consistent customer service. Crew members are trained to greet customers with a smile, take orders accurately, and serve food quickly and efficiently. This focus on consistent service has helped McDonald's build a reputation for reliability and convenience.

By maintaining consistency across its menu, restaurant design, and customer service, McDonald's has created a strong, recognizable brand that customers trust and rely on for a familiar, satisfying experience.

Apple

Apple, the iconic technology company, is another brand that exemplifies the Law of Consistency (Experience). From its products to its retail stores, Apple has cultivated a consistent brand experience that is instantly recognizable and deeply appealing to its loyal customer base.

One of the hallmarks of Apple's consistency is its product design. Apple products, from iPhones and iPads to MacBooks and Apple Watches, share a distinctive aesthetic that is sleek, minimalist, and user-friendly. This consistency in design makes Apple products instantly recognizable and creates a sense of familiarity and trust among customers.

Apple's retail stores are another key touchpoint where the brand maintains a consistent experience. Apple Stores are known for their clean, spacious layouts, knowledgeable staff, and hands-on product demonstrations. Customers can expect the same high-quality service and immersive experience whether they visit an Apple Store in New York, London, or Tokyo.

In addition to its physical consistency, Apple also maintains consistency in its digital experiences. The company's website, mobile apps, and software interfaces share a common design language and user experience that is intuitive, streamlined, and visually appealing. This consistency makes it easy for customers to navigate Apple's ecosystem and reinforces the brand's commitment to simplicity and user-centricity.

Apple's consistency extends to its marketing and messaging as well. The company is known for its iconic advertising campaigns, which often feature clean, minimalist visuals and emotive storytelling. These campaigns consistently communicate Apple's core values of innovation, creativity, and empowerment, reinforcing the brand's identity and appeal.

By maintaining consistency across its product design, retail experiences, digital touchpoints, and marketing, Apple has built one of the world's most valuable and recognizable brands. This consistency has helped Apple cultivate a fiercely loyal customer base and establish itself as a leader in the technology industry.

In conclusion, by embracing the Law of Consistency (Experience), brands can build trust, familiarity, and loyalty among their customers. By delivering a consistent experience across all touchpoints, brands can strengthen their identity, differentiate themselves from competitors, and drive long-term success in the marketplace.

* * *

21

The Law of Interactivity

In the modern branding landscape, engaging customers and fostering meaningful relationships is more important than ever. The Law of Interactivity states that brands should design experiences that encourage active participation and dialogue with customers, creating a sense of engagement, connection, and loyalty. By embracing interactivity, brands can transform passive consumers into active participants, driving deeper emotional connections and long-term brand advocacy.

The Benefits of Interactivity in Branding

Incorporating interactivity into brand experiences offers several key benefits:

1. **Increased engagement:** Interactive experiences capture customers' attention and encourage them to spend more time and effort engaging with the brand, leading to increased brand recall and loyalty.
2. **Deeper emotional connections:** By actively participating in brand experiences, customers forge stronger emotional bonds with the brand, as they feel more invested in the relationship and valued by the company.
3. **Valuable customer insights:** Interactive experiences provide brands with opportunities to gather valuable data and insights about their

customer's preferences, behaviours, and needs, which can inform future marketing and product development strategies.
4. **Differentiation from competitors:** In a crowded marketplace, interactive experiences can help brands stand out and differentiate themselves from competitors by offering unique, memorable, and engaging touchpoints.
5. **Increased brand advocacy:** When customers have positive, interactive experiences with a brand, they are more likely to share those experiences with others, driving word-of-mouth marketing and brand advocacy.

Strategies for Implementing Interactivity in Brand Experiences

1. **Gamification:** Incorporate game-like elements into brand experiences, such as challenges, rewards, and leaderboards, to encourage active participation and engagement. Gamification can be applied to various touchpoints, including websites, mobile apps, and in-store experiences.
2. **User-generated content:** Encourage customers to create and share their own content related to the brand, such as photos, videos, or reviews. This not only increases engagement but also provides valuable social proof and authentic content for the brand to leverage.
3. **Personalization:** Use data and technology to create personalized, interactive experiences tailored to individual customers' preferences and needs. This can include personalized product recommendations, customized content, or interactive tools that help customers make informed decisions.
4. **Co-creation opportunities:** Invite customers to participate in the brand's creative process, such as voting on new product designs, suggesting ideas for marketing campaigns, or even collaborating on limited-edition products. Co-creation fosters a sense of ownership and investment in the brand.
5. **Interactive storytelling:** Develop immersive, interactive brand narratives that allow customers to explore and engage with the brand's story on their own terms. This can include interactive videos, choose-your-

own-adventure style content, or augmented reality experiences that bring the brand story to life.
6. **Social media engagement:** Leverage social media platforms to create interactive experiences that encourage conversation, sharing, and engagement. This can include polls, quizzes, live Q&A sessions, or hashtag campaigns that invite customers to participate and connect with the brand and each other.
7. **Experiential events:** Design interactive, immersive events that allow customers to engage with the brand in a meaningful way. These can include product demonstrations, workshops, pop-up experiences, or community gatherings that foster a sense of connection and belonging.

Sephora

Sephora, the global beauty retailer, has embraced interactivity as a key component of its brand experience, both online and in-store. By offering a range of interactive tools and experiences, Sephora encourages customers to actively engage with the brand and its products.

One of Sephora's most successful interactive features is its "Virtual Artist" tool, available on the brand's mobile app and website. This tool uses augmented reality technology to allow customers to virtually try on different makeup products, from lipsticks and eyeshadows to foundation and blush. By uploading a photo or using their device's camera, customers can see how different products look on their own faces, making it easier to find the perfect shades and styles. This interactive experience not only provides a practical benefit for customers but also creates a sense of play and experimentation that encourages deeper engagement with the brand.

In-store, Sephora offers interactive touchscreens and digital displays that allow customers to access product information, read reviews, and even receive personalized recommendations based on their preferences. These interactive elements create a more immersive and engaging shopping experience, encouraging customers to spend more time exploring and discovering new products.

Sephora also leverages interactivity through its "Beauty Insider" loyalty program, which offers members exclusive access to interactive experiences, such as live chat with beauty experts, virtual beauty classes, and members-only events. These interactive touchpoints foster a sense of community and belonging among Sephora's most engaged customers, driving long-term loyalty and advocacy.

Warby Parker

Warby Parker, the innovative eyewear retailer, has built its brand on a foundation of interactivity and customer engagement. By offering a range of interactive tools and experiences, Warby Parker has made the process of buying glasses more engaging, convenient, and personalized.

One of Warby Parker's most iconic interactive features is its "Home Try-On" program, which allows customers to select up to five frames from the company's website, which are then shipped to their homes for free. Customers have five days to try on the glasses, share photos with friends and family, and decide which frames they like best before sending them back. This interactive experience not only makes it easier for customers to find the perfect frames but also creates a sense of excitement and anticipation around the purchasing process.

In addition to the Home Try-On program, Warby Parker also offers an interactive "Virtual Try-On" tool on its website and mobile app. This tool uses augmented reality technology to allow customers to see how different frames look on their own faces, making it easier to narrow down their choices and find the perfect style. This interactive feature not only provides a practical benefit but also creates a sense of fun and engagement that sets Warby Parker apart from traditional eyewear retailers.

Warby Parker also leverages interactivity through its social media presence, regularly engaging with customers through polls, quizzes, and user-generated content campaigns. By encouraging customers to share their own photos and experiences with Warby Parker products, the brand fosters a sense of community and authenticity that resonates with its target audience.

Finally, Warby Parker's in-store experience is designed to be highly interactive, with knowledgeable staff, digital displays, and even photo booths that allow customers to capture and share their new look. These interactive elements create a memorable and engaging shopping experience that reinforces Warby Parker's brand identity and values.

In conclusion, by embracing the Law of Interactivity, brands can create dynamic, engaging experiences that transform customers from passive observers to active participants. Through a combination of gamification, personalization, co-creation, and immersive storytelling, brands can forge deeper emotional connections, gather valuable insights, and drive long-term loyalty and advocacy.

* * *

22

The Law of Personalization

In today's highly competitive and customer-centric market, brands that understand and cater to their customers' unique needs and preferences are more likely to succeed. The Law of Personalization states that brands should tailor their experiences, products, and communications to individual customers' preferences, needs, and behaviors, creating a more relevant, engaging, and memorable experience. By embracing personalization, brands can forge stronger emotional connections, increase customer satisfaction, and drive long-term loyalty.

The Power of Personalization in Branding

Personalization offers several key benefits for brands:

1. **Increased relevance:** By tailoring experiences to individual customers, brands can deliver more relevant content, recommendations, and offerings, increasing the likelihood of engagement and conversion.
2. **Enhanced customer satisfaction:** Personalized experiences demonstrate that a brand understands and values its customers, leading to higher levels of satisfaction and positive sentiment.
3. **Improved customer loyalty:** When customers feel understood and

valued by a brand, they are more likely to develop a strong emotional connection and remain loyal over time.
4. **Increased customer lifetime value:** Personalized experiences can lead to higher engagement, more frequent purchases, and increased spending, ultimately driving greater customer lifetime value.
5. **Competitive differentiation:** In a crowded marketplace, personalization can help brands stand out by delivering unique, tailored experiences that set them apart from competitors.

Strategies for Implementing Personalization in Branding

1. **Collect and analyze customer data:** To deliver personalized experiences, brands must first gather and analyze data about their customers' preferences, behaviours, and interactions. This can include demographic information, purchase history, browsing behaviour, and social media activity.
2. **Segment customers based on shared characteristics:** Use customer data to segment audiences based on common attributes, such as age, location, interests, or purchase behaviour. This allows brands to tailor their messaging and offerings to specific groups of customers.
3. **Use machine learning and AI:** Leverage machine learning algorithms and artificial intelligence to analyze customer data and deliver personalized recommendations, content, and experiences in real time.
4. **Personalize across touchpoints:** Implement personalization across various customer touchpoints, including websites, mobile apps, email campaigns, social media interactions, and in-store experiences.
5. **Offer customization options:** Give customers the ability to customize their products or experiences, such as allowing them to select specific features, colors, or designs. This creates a sense of ownership and personal connection with the brand.
6. **Deliver targeted content and recommendations:** Use customer data to deliver personalized content, product recommendations, and promotions that align with individual customers' interests and needs.

7. **Continuously test and optimize:** Regularly assess the effectiveness of personalization efforts and use A/B testing to refine and optimize strategies over time. Continuously gather customer feedback and adapt personalization approaches based on insights and results.

Amazon

Amazon, the global e-commerce giant, has mastered the art of personalization, delivering highly tailored experiences to its millions of customers worldwide. By collecting and analyzing vast amounts of customer data, Amazon has created a personalized shopping experience that keeps customers engaged, satisfied, and loyal to the brand.

One of the most prominent examples of Amazon's personalization is its product recommendation engine. When a customer visits Amazon's website or app, they are greeted with a personalized homepage featuring products that are likely to be of interest based on their browsing and purchase history. These recommendations are generated using sophisticated machine learning algorithms that analyze a wide range of data points, including past purchases, product searches, and even the behaviour of similar customers.

Amazon also leverages personalization in its email marketing campaigns, sending customers targeted promotions and product suggestions based on their interests and preferences. These personalized emails help to drive engagement and encourage repeat purchases, as customers are more likely to respond positively to offers that are relevant to their needs.

Another example of Amazon's personalization is its "Subscribe & Save" program, which allows customers to set up recurring deliveries of their favourite products at discounted prices. By analyzing customer purchase patterns, Amazon can predict when a customer is likely to run out of a particular product and send a reminder email to encourage them to reorder, creating a seamless and convenient shopping experience.

Sephora

Sephora, the global beauty retailer, has also embraced personalization as a key component of its brand experience. By collecting customer data through its Beauty Insider loyalty program and online interactions, Sephora delivers personalized product recommendations, content, and experiences that cater to each customer's unique needs and preferences.

One of Sephora's most effective personalization tools is its "Beauty Insider Community" platform, which allows customers to create profiles, share their favorite products, and connect with other beauty enthusiasts. Based on a customer's profile information, product ratings, and interactions within the community, Sephora can deliver highly targeted product recommendations and content that aligns with their interests and needs.

Sephora also leverages personalization in its email marketing campaigns, sending customers targeted promotions, product suggestions, and educational content based on their purchase history, skin type, and beauty preferences. These personalized emails help to foster a sense of connection and relevance, encouraging customers to engage with the brand and try new products.

In-store, Sephora offers personalized consultations with beauty experts who can recommend products and techniques based on a customer's individual needs and preferences. By providing this level of personalized attention, Sephora creates a memorable and engaging shopping experience that sets it apart from other beauty retailers.

Finally, Sephora's "Color IQ" technology takes personalization to the next level by scanning a customer's skin tone and providing a unique Color IQ number that can be used to find perfectly matched foundation, concealer, and lip colors. This innovative tool demonstrates Sephora's commitment to delivering highly personalized solutions that cater to each customer's unique beauty needs.

In conclusion, by embracing the Law of Personalization, brands can create experiences that resonate with individual customers on a deeper level. Through data-driven insights, targeted content, and customized offerings, brands can forge stronger emotional connections, increase customer satisfaction, and drive long-term loyalty and advocacy. As customer expectations for personalized experiences continue to grow, brands that master the art of personalization will be well-positioned for success in the future.

* * *

23

The Law of Emotional Connection

In the world of branding, creating an emotional connection with customers is paramount to building lasting relationships and fostering brand loyalty. The Law of Emotional Connection states that brands should strive to create deep, meaningful connections with their customers by tapping into their desires, aspirations, and values. By doing so, brands can transcend mere transactions and establish themselves as an integral part of their customers' lives.

Why Emotional Connections Matter

Emotions play a crucial role in decision-making and brand perception. When customers form an emotional connection with a brand, they are more likely to:

1. Remember the brand and its message
2. Choose the brand over the competitors
3. Advocate for the brand and recommend it to others
4. Forgive the brand for occasional missteps or shortcomings
5. Engage with the brand on a deeper level

Strategies for Building Emotional Connections

1. **Understand your customers:** To create an emotional connection, brands must first understand their customers on a deep level. This includes their needs, desires, aspirations, values, and pain points. Conduct research, gather feedback, and engage in active listening to gain insights into your customers' emotional drivers.
2. **Align with customer values:** Identify the values that are important to your target audience and align your brand with those values. This can include a commitment to sustainability, social responsibility, inclusivity, or other causes that resonate with your customers. By demonstrating shared values, brands can create a sense of kinship and emotional connection.
3. **Tell authentic stories:** Use storytelling to create an emotional narrative around your brand. Share stories that highlight your brand's purpose, values, and impact on customers' lives. Authentic, relatable stories can evoke emotions and create a sense of connection between the brand and its customers.
4. **Evoke positive emotions:** Focus on evoking positive emotions through your branding efforts, such as joy, excitement, inspiration, or a sense of belonging. Use imagery, language, and experiences that elicit these emotions and create a positive association with your brand.
5. **Create memorable moments:** Design experiences and interactions that create memorable, emotionally charged moments for your customers. This can include surprise and delight initiatives, personalized gestures, or immersive experiences that leave a lasting impression.
6. **Show empathy and understanding:** Demonstrate empathy and understanding towards your customers' challenges, struggles, and aspirations. Show that your brand is there to support them, celebrate their successes, and help them overcome obstacles. This can create a sense of emotional connection and loyalty.
7. **Foster community and belonging:** Create a sense of community and belonging around your brand, connecting customers with shared in-

terests, values, or experiences. This can include online communities, events, or initiatives that bring customers together and create a sense of camaraderie and emotional connection.

Nordstrom

Nordstrom, a leading fashion retailer, has built a strong emotional connection with its customers through exceptional customer service and personalized experiences. The brand is renowned for its commitment to going above and beyond to satisfy customers' needs and desires.

One of the key ways Nordstrom creates emotional connections is through its personalized shopping experiences. Sales associates, known as "Personal Stylists," work closely with customers to understand their individual style preferences, body types, and fashion needs. They provide tailored recommendations, help with outfit curation, and offer honest advice, creating a sense of trust and emotional connection between the customer and the brand.

Nordstrom's exceptional customer service also contributes to building emotional connections. The company empowers its employees to make decisions that prioritize customer satisfaction, even if it means bending the rules or going the extra mile. This customer-centric approach creates memorable, emotionally positive experiences that foster a deep sense of loyalty.

Furthermore, Nordstrom's in-store experiences are designed to create a sense of luxury, comfort, and enjoyment. From the elegant store design and attentive staff to the high-quality products and personalized touches, every aspect of the shopping experience is crafted to evoke positive emotions and create a lasting emotional connection.

By consistently delivering personalized, emotionally satisfying shopping experiences and prioritizing customer service, Nordstrom has established a strong emotional bond with its customers, setting itself apart in the competitive retail landscape.

By leveraging the Law of Emotional Connection, brands can create deep, meaningful relationships with their customers that go beyond mere transactions. By understanding customers' emotional drivers, aligning with their values, and creating memorable, emotionally charged experiences, brands can establish themselves as an integral part of their customers' lives, fostering lasting loyalty and advocacy.

* * *

24

The Law of Building Relationships (With Customers)

In today's competitive business landscape, building strong, lasting relationships with customers is more important than ever. The Law of Building Relationships states that a brand's success is directly proportional to the strength and depth of the relationships it cultivates with its customers. This law is rooted in the understanding that customers are not just transactions but individuals with unique needs, preferences, and emotions.

Why Building Relationships Matters

Building strong customer relationships offers numerous benefits for brands:

1. **Increased loyalty:** When customers feel valued and connected to a brand, they are more likely to remain loyal over time, even in the face of competition or challenges.
2. **Higher lifetime value:** Strong relationships lead to repeat business, up-selling, and cross-selling opportunities, increasing the overall lifetime value of each customer.

3. **Positive word-of-mouth:** Satisfied customers who feel a strong connection to a brand are more likely to recommend it to others, generating valuable word-of-mouth marketing.
4. **Valuable feedback and insights:** Close relationships with customers provide brands with a wealth of feedback and insights that can inform product development, service improvements, and marketing strategies.
5. **Competitive advantage:** In a crowded marketplace, strong customer relationships can differentiate a brand and provide a sustainable competitive advantage.

Strategies for Building Customer Relationships

Building strong customer relationships requires a holistic, customer-centric approach that prioritizes empathy, communication, and value creation. Here are some key strategies for building lasting relationships:

1. **Understand your customers:** Invest time and resources into understanding your customers' needs, preferences, and pain points. Use customer data, feedback, and research to gain a deep understanding of who they are and what they value.
2. **Personalize the experience:** Use your understanding of individual customers to personalize their experiences with your brand. This can include tailored product recommendations, customized communications, and personalized service.
3. **Provide exceptional service:** Consistently deliver high-quality, responsive, and empathetic customer service across all touchpoints. Train your staff to prioritize customer needs and go above and beyond to resolve issues and create positive experiences.
4. **Foster emotional connections:** Move beyond transactional interactions and strive to create emotional connections with customers. This can involve storytelling, shared values, and experiences that resonate on a deeper level.
5. **Engage in ongoing communication:** Maintain regular, two-way com-

munication with customers across multiple channels. This can include email, social media, phone, and in-person interactions. Show customers that you value their input and are committed to meeting their needs.
6. **Show appreciation:** Regularly express gratitude and appreciation for your customers' business and loyalty. This can involve personalized thank-you notes, exclusive offers, or special events for loyal customers.
7. **Create a community:** Foster a sense of community among your customers by creating opportunities for them to connect with each other and with your brand. This can include online forums, in-person events, or social media groups centered around shared interests or values.

Examples of Brands

That Excel at Building Relationships Several brands have successfully built strong, lasting relationships with their customers. Here are a few examples:

1. **Zappos:** The online shoe retailer is renowned for its exceptional customer service, including free shipping and returns, 24/7 customer support, and personalized recommendations. Zappos prioritizes customer satisfaction above all else, creating a loyal following.
2. **Starbucks:** The coffee giant has built a strong sense of community among its customers through personalized experiences, a loyalty program, and a commitment to social and environmental responsibility. Starbucks stores serve as social hubs, fostering connection and belonging.
3. **Patagonia:** The outdoor clothing brand has cultivated a dedicated customer base through its commitment to environmental sustainability and activism. Patagonia regularly communicates its values and engages customers in its mission, creating a strong sense of shared purpose.
4. **Sephora:** The beauty retailer has built strong relationships with customers through personalized recommendations, in-store events and classes, and a robust loyalty program. Sephora's knowledgeable staff and immersive store experiences create a sense of connection and

community.

Building strong, lasting relationships with customers is essential for creating a positive brand experience and driving long-term success. By prioritizing empathy, personalization, communication, and value creation, brands can cultivate deep, emotional connections with their customers that lead to increased loyalty, advocacy, and growth. In a world where customers have more choices than ever, the brands that invest in building authentic, mutually beneficial relationships will be the ones that thrive.

* * *

25

The Law of Community

In the era of social media and digital connectivity, brands that foster a strong sense of community among their customers are more likely to thrive. The Law of Community states that a brand's success is directly linked to its ability to create, nurture, and engage a community of loyal customers who share common values, interests, and experiences. This law recognizes that humans are inherently social beings who crave connection, belonging, and shared purpose.

Why Community Matters

Building a strong brand community offers numerous benefits:

1. **Loyalty and advocacy:** When customers feel a strong sense of belonging and connection to a brand community, they are more likely to remain loyal and become passionate advocates for the brand.
2. **User-generated content:** Engaged communities often create and share their own content, such as reviews, testimonials, and social media posts, providing valuable social proof and authentic marketing material for the brand.
3. **Feedback and insights:** Brand communities serve as a valuable source

of feedback, ideas, and insights that can help brands improve their products, services, and overall customer experience.
4. **Increased customer lifetime value:** Customers who are part of a brand community tend to have a higher lifetime value, as they are more likely to make repeat purchases, upgrade to premium offerings, and recommend the brand to others.
5. **Competitive advantage:** A strong, engaged community can differentiate a brand from its competitors and create a sustainable competitive advantage.

Strategies for Building Brand Communities

Building a thriving brand community requires a deliberate, customer-centric approach that prioritizes authentic engagement, shared values, and mutual benefit. Here are some key strategies for building strong brand communities:

1. **Define your community's purpose:** Clearly articulate the shared values, interests, and goals that unite your brand community. This purpose should align with your brand's mission and resonate with your target audience.
2. **Provide a platform for engagement:** Create digital and/or physical spaces where community members can connect, interact, and share their experiences. This can include online forums, social media groups, or in-person events.
3. **Encourage user-generated content:** Empower your community members to create and share their own content by providing prompts, challenges, and incentives. Showcase and celebrate the best user-generated content across your brand's channels.
4. **Foster meaningful interactions:** Facilitate meaningful conversations and connections among community members by asking questions, sparking debates, and encouraging members to support one another.
5. **Offer exclusive benefits:** Provide exclusive perks, experiences, and opportunities to community members, such as early access to new

products, special discounts, or invitations to VIP events.
6. **Recognize and reward engagement:** Acknowledge and reward your most active and valuable community members through public recognition, special privileges, or loyalty programs.
7. **Lead with authenticity and transparency:** Build trust and credibility with your community by being authentic, transparent, and responsive in your interactions. Address concerns, admit mistakes, and involve the community in key decisions when appropriate.

Examples of Brands with Strong Communities

Several brands have successfully cultivated thriving communities that drive loyalty, advocacy, and growth:

1. **Lululemon:** The athletic apparel brand has built a strong community of yoga and fitness enthusiasts through a combination of in-store classes, local events, and online engagement. Lululemon's brand ambassadors, who are often local fitness instructors or influencers, play a key role in fostering connections and inspiring the community.
2. **Sephora:** The beauty retailer's Beauty Insider Community is a vibrant online platform where makeup and skincare enthusiasts can connect, share tips and reviews, and get expert advice from Sephora staff. The community helps Sephora build trust, gather valuable feedback, and drive loyalty among its most engaged customers.
3. **Harley-Davidson:** The iconic motorcycle brand has one of the most devoted and passionate brand communities in the world, united by a shared love of the open road and a rebellious spirit. The Harley Owners Group (H.O.G.) organizes rides, rallies, and charity events that bring Harley enthusiasts together and reinforce the brand's tight-knit community.
4. **Salesforce:** The cloud-based software company has built a strong com-

munity of developers, administrators, and users who share knowledge, collaborate on projects, and provide feedback to improve the Salesforce platform. The Salesforce Community, which includes online forums, local user groups, and the annual Dreamforce conference, is a key driver of the brand's success and customer loyalty.

Building a strong brand community is essential for creating a memorable, engaging brand experience that drives loyalty, advocacy, and long-term success. By fostering meaningful connections, shared values, and mutual benefit among customers, brands can cultivate a sustainable competitive advantage and thrive in an increasingly connected world. The Law of Community recognizes that in today's landscape, the brands that bring people together around a common purpose will be the ones that win hearts, minds, and wallets.

* * *

V

Part 05—Brand Communication

26

The Law of Clarity

In the context of brand communication, The Law of Clarity emphasizes the importance of conveying a clear, concise, and easily understandable message to the target audience. Clarity is essential for effective brand communication, as it enables consumers to quickly grasp the key benefits, values, and unique selling propositions of a brand.

In today's fast-paced, information-saturated world, consumers are bombarded with countless marketing messages every day. To cut through the noise and capture the attention of their target audience, brands must prioritize clarity in their communication. Clarity involves simplifying complex ideas, avoiding jargon, and communicating in a straightforward manner that resonates with the intended audience.

The Law of Clarity is rooted in the understanding that consumers have limited time and attention spans. They are more likely to engage with and remember brands that communicate their message in a clear, concise, and memorable way. When a brand's communication is ambiguous, convoluted, or confusing, consumers are likely to disengage or misinterpret the intended message.

To effectively implement The Law of Clarity, brands must first have a deep understanding of their target audience. This includes knowledge of their audience's demographics, psychographics, and communication preferences. By tailoring their messaging to the specific needs and preferences of their audience, brands can ensure that their communication is clear and relevant.

Simplicity is a key aspect of clarity in brand communication. Brands should strive to distill their message down to its core essence, focusing on the most important benefits and values that differentiate them from competitors. By using simple, straightforward language and avoiding industry jargon, brands can ensure that their message is easily understood by their target audience.

Visual clarity is also crucial in brand communication. The use of clear, high-quality images, infographics, and videos can help convey complex ideas in a more easily digestible format. Brands should ensure that their visual communication is consistent with their overall brand identity and effectively reinforces their key messaging.

Consistency is another important aspect of clarity in brand communication. Brands should maintain a consistent tone, voice, and messaging across all communication channels, from advertising and social media to customer service interactions. Consistency helps reinforce the brand's identity and values, making it easier for consumers to recognize and remember the brand.

For example, Apple is known for its clear, simple, and consistent brand communication. The company's messaging focuses on the key benefits of its products, such as ease of use, design, and innovation. Apple's visual communication is also highly consistent, with a minimalist aesthetic that reinforces the brand's focus on simplicity and clarity.

Another example is Dollar Shave Club, a subscription-based razor company that disrupted the shaving industry with its clear, humorous, and relatable brand communication. The company's messaging focuses on the simple value proposition of delivering high-quality razors at a low cost, directly to the consumer's door. Dollar Shave Club's communication is consistent across all channels, with a tone that is both funny and straightforward, resonating with its target audience of budget-conscious, no-nonsense consumers.

Here are a few more examples:

1. **Uber:** Uber, the ride-hailing service, has built its brand communication around a clear and simple message: "Tap a button, get a ride." This con-

cise statement effectively communicates the core value proposition of Uber – the ease and convenience of ordering a ride through a smartphone app. Uber's communication is consistently clear across all channels, from its app interface to its advertising campaigns, emphasizing the simplicity and reliability of its service.

2. **Mailchimp:** Mailchimp, an email marketing and automation platform, is known for its clear and approachable brand communication. The company's messaging focuses on simplifying the complex world of email marketing, making it accessible to businesses of all sizes. Mailchimp's website features clear, concise explanations of its features and benefits, along with simple, step-by-step guides to help users get started. The brand's communication is consistently friendly, humorous, and jargon-free, reinforcing its commitment to clarity and simplicity.

3. **Slack:** Slack, the popular team collaboration and messaging tool, has built its brand communication around the idea of simplifying workplace communication. The company's messaging emphasizes how Slack streamlines communication, making it easier for teams to collaborate and get work done. Slack's website and marketing materials feature clear, concise explanations of its features, along with real-world examples of how the platform can be used to improve productivity. The brand's communication is consistently clear, focusing on the benefits of using Slack for team collaboration.

4. **Southwest Airlines:** Southwest Airlines, the American low-cost carrier, is known for its clear and straightforward brand communication. The company's messaging focuses on its core value proposition of offering low fares, friendly service, and a simple, no-frills flying experience. Southwest's communication is consistently clear and transparent, with easy-to-understand pricing, no hidden fees, and a focus on customer service. The brand's humorous and relatable tone also reinforces its commitment to clarity and simplicity in air travel.

5. **Mint:** Mint, the personal finance and budgeting app, has built its brand communication around the idea of making financial management clear, simple, and accessible to everyone. The company's messaging focuses

on how Mint helps users take control of their finances by providing a clear, comprehensive view of their financial situation. Mint's website and app feature clear, easy-to-understand visualizations of users' spending, income, and budgets, along with personalized insights and recommendations. The brand's communication is consistently clear and jargon-free, empowering users to make informed financial decisions.

In conclusion, The Law of Clarity emphasizes the importance of conveying a clear, concise, and easily understandable message in brand communication. By prioritizing simplicity, consistency, and tailoring their messaging to their target audience, brands can cut through the noise and effectively communicate their unique value proposition. Clarity in communication helps build trust, credibility, and memorability, ultimately fostering strong relationships between brands and their customers.

* * *

27

The Law of Emotional Appeal

In the realm of brand communication, The Law of Emotional Appeal states that brands that effectively connect with their audience on an emotional level are more likely to foster strong, lasting relationships with their customers. Emotional appeal goes beyond merely communicating the functional benefits of a product or service; it taps into the deeper psychological needs and desires of the target audience.

The power of emotional appeal lies in its ability to create a bond between the brand and the consumer. When a brand successfully evokes positive emotions, such as happiness, excitement, or a sense of belonging, it becomes more memorable and influential in the minds of its audience. Consumers are more likely to engage with, trust, and remain loyal to brands that resonate with them on an emotional level.

To effectively implement The Law of Emotional Appeal, brands must first understand their target audience's emotional needs and motivations. This requires deep insight into the customer's psyche, including their aspirations, fears, and values. By conducting thorough market research and creating detailed buyer personas, brands can identify the emotional triggers that will resonate with their audience.

Once the emotional needs of the audience are identified, brands can craft their messaging and storytelling to address these needs. This can be achieved through various communication channels, such as advertising, social media, content marketing, and experiential marketing. The key is to create a consistent emotional narrative that aligns with the brand's values and purpose.

For example, Nike's "Just Do It" campaign has been successful for decades because it taps into the emotional desire for self-empowerment and achievement. The campaign inspires consumers to push past their limits and embrace their inner athlete, creating a strong emotional connection with the brand.

Similarly, Dove's "Real Beauty" campaign resonated with women worldwide by challenging traditional beauty standards and promoting self-acceptance. By addressing the emotional need for self-esteem and body positivity, Dove created a powerful emotional bond with its audience.

However, it is essential for brands to ensure that their emotional appeal is authentic and aligned with their core values. Inauthentic emotional appeals can backfire, leading to consumer distrust and negative brand perception. Brands must genuinely embody the emotions they promote and consistently deliver on their emotional promise across all touchpoints.

Moreover, brands should strive to create emotional appeals that are distinctive and differentiated from their competitors. In a crowded market, brands that can tap into unique emotional needs and create a strong emotional connection with their audience are more likely to stand out and build a loyal customer base.

Airbnb

Airbnb, the online marketplace for unique accommodations, has successfully leveraged emotional appeal in its brand communication. The company's messaging focuses on the emotional desire for belonging, adventure, and authentic experiences.

Airbnb's "Belong Anywhere" campaign perfectly encapsulates the emotional appeal of the brand. The campaign showcases real stories of travellers and hosts from around the world, highlighting the personal connections and unique experiences that Airbnb facilitates. By emphasizing the idea of belonging and the transformative power of travel, Airbnb taps into the emotional yearning for exploration and human connection.

The brand's communication also emphasizes the notion of living like a local, appealing to the emotional desire for authentic experiences. Airbnb's website and social media feature captivating images and stories that inspire wanderlust and evoke the excitement of immersing oneself in new cultures and communities.

Moreover, Airbnb's "Night At" series, which offers once-in-a-lifetime experiences like sleeping in the Great Wall of China or the Louvre, further amplifies the emotional appeal of the brand. These extraordinary experiences create a sense of exclusivity and adventure, emotionally connecting with consumers who seek unique and memorable travel moments.

By consistently communicating the emotional benefits of belonging, authenticity, and adventure, Airbnb has built a strong emotional bond with its audience, fostering loyalty and advocacy among its users.

Subaru

Subaru, the Japanese automaker, has effectively leveraged emotional appeal in its brand communication, particularly in the North American market. The company's messaging focuses on the emotional values of safety, reliability, and love.

Subaru's "Love" campaign, which has been running for over a decade, is a prime example of emotional appeal in action. The campaign features heartwarming stories that showcase the emotional connection between Subaru owners and their vehicles. From families going on adventures together to loyal Subaru owners passing down their beloved cars to the next generation, the campaign emphasizes the idea that Subaru is more than just a car—it's a trusted companion that becomes part of the family.

The brand's communication also heavily emphasizes safety, tapping into the emotional need for protection and peace of mind. Subaru's advertisements often feature real-life stories of how the brand's advanced safety features have saved lives or prevented accidents. By highlighting the emotional benefit of keeping loved ones safe, Subaru creates a strong emotional connection with its audience, particularly with families and safety-conscious consumers.

Furthermore, Subaru's commitment to environmental sustainability and charitable causes adds another layer of emotional appeal to the brand. The company's "Share the Love" event, which donates a portion of sales to various charities, resonates with consumers who value corporate social responsibility and want to support brands that make a positive impact.

Through its consistent focus on love, safety, and social responsibility, Subaru has built a strong emotional bond with its audience. The brand's communication effectively taps into the emotional needs and values of its target market, fostering loyalty and advocacy among Subaru owners.

In conclusion, The Law of Emotional Appeal emphasizes the importance of connecting with consumers on a deeper, emotional level. By understanding their audience's emotional needs, crafting authentic and compelling emotional narratives, and consistently delivering on their emotional promise, brands can build strong, lasting relationships with their customers. Emotional appeal is a powerful tool in brand communication, enabling brands to differentiate themselves, foster loyalty, and create a meaningful impact in the lives of their audience.

* * *

28

The Law of Thought Leadership

In the context of brand communication, The Law of Thought Leadership emphasizes the importance of establishing a brand as an authority and expert in its industry or niche. Thought leadership involves sharing valuable insights, knowledge, and opinions that demonstrate a deep understanding of the industry and provide solutions to the challenges faced by the target audience.

The Law of Thought Leadership recognizes that in today's competitive marketplace, it is not enough for brands to simply promote their products or services. Consumers are increasingly seeking brands that can provide them with valuable information, educate them, and help them make informed decisions. By establishing themselves as thought leaders, brands can differentiate themselves from competitors, build trust and credibility, and foster long-term relationships with their target audiences.

To effectively implement The Law of Thought Leadership, brands must develop a strategic content marketing plan that focuses on creating and distributing high-quality, informative, and engaging content. This content should address the pain points, challenges, and aspirations of the target audience, providing them with actionable insights and solutions.

One key aspect of thought leadership is to identify the unique perspective and expertise that the brand can offer. This involves a deep understanding of the industry landscape, trends, and challenges, as well as the brand's own strengths and unique value proposition. By leveraging this knowledge, brands can create content that sets them apart from competitors and positions them as go-to resources in their field.

Thought leadership content can take various forms, such as blog posts, whitepapers, e-books, webinars, podcasts, and speaking engagements. The key is to create content that is valuable, relevant, and shareable, helping to establish the brand as a trusted source of information and insights.

Consistency is another important aspect of thought leadership. Brands must commit to regularly creating and sharing high-quality content that aligns with their overall brand messaging and values. This helps to reinforce the brand's expertise and authority over time, building a loyal following of engaged audiences.

Thought leadership also involves actively engaging with the target audience and industry peers. This can include participating in industry events, forums, and social media discussions, as well as collaborating with other thought leaders and influencers. By actively participating in the industry conversation, brands can further establish their expertise, gain valuable insights, and build relationships with key stakeholders.

Patagonia

Patagonia is an excellent example of a brand that effectively demonstrates The Law of Thought Leadership through its various initiatives and commitment to environmental sustainability.

Patagonia's Thought Leadership Initiatives:

1. **Patagonia Action Works:** Patagonia launched this digital platform to connect individuals with local grassroots organizations working to protect the environment. By providing resources, funding, and a network for environmental activists, Patagonia positions itself as a leader in environmental advocacy and empowers its customers to make a difference.

2. **The Footprint Chronicles:** Patagonia is transparent about its supply chain and environmental impact through this initiative. By sharing detailed information about the materials, manufacturing processes, and environmental footprint of its products, Patagonia demonstrates its commitment to sustainability and encourages other companies to follow suit.
3. **Worn Wear:** This program encourages customers to repair, reuse, and recycle their Patagonia garments, reducing waste and promoting a circular economy. By offering repair services and selling second-hand clothing, Patagonia shows its dedication to extending the life of its products and reducing environmental impact.
4. **1% for the Planet:** Patagonia co-founded this initiative, which commits the company to donating 1% of its annual sales to environmental organizations. By setting an example and encouraging other businesses to do the same, Patagonia demonstrates its leadership in corporate social responsibility.
5. **Patagonia's Blog and Films:** Patagonia regularly creates content that educates and inspires its audience about environmental issues, outdoor activities, and sustainable living. Through its blog, films, and other content, Patagonia shares valuable insights and stories that position the brand as a thought leader in its industry.

IBM

IBM's Thought Leadership Initiatives:

1. **IBM Institute for Business Value:** This think tank produces research and thought leadership content on a wide range of business and technology topics. By sharing insights, benchmarks, and best practices, IBM helps organizations stay informed and make data-driven decisions.
2. **IBM Watson:** As a pioneer in artificial intelligence, IBM has positioned

itself as a thought leader in AI through its Watson platform. By showcasing the potential applications and benefits of AI across industries, IBM demonstrates its expertise and drives innovation in this field.

3. **IBM Garage:** This global network of innovation centers brings together IBM experts, business leaders, and developers to co-create solutions using emerging technologies. By fostering collaboration and knowledge-sharing, IBM Garage positions the company as a thought leader in digital transformation and innovation.

4. **IBM Think Conference:** This annual event brings together business and technology leaders from around the world to explore the latest trends, challenges, and opportunities in the industry. By hosting this influential conference, IBM reinforces its position as a thought leader and facilitates valuable conversations and connections.

5. **IBM's Thought Leadership Content:** IBM regularly publishes whitepapers, reports, and articles that provide insights and guidance on various business and technology topics. By sharing its expertise and perspectives, IBM helps organizations navigate complex challenges and make informed decisions.

Through these initiatives, both Patagonia and IBM demonstrate their commitment to thought leadership in their respective industries. By consistently providing valuable insights, driving innovation, and addressing the needs and challenges of their audiences, these brands establish themselves as trusted authorities and partners. Their thought leadership efforts not only benefit their customers and communities but also contribute to the overall advancement and sustainability of their industries.

In conclusion, The Law of Thought Leadership underscores the importance of establishing a brand as an authority and expert in its industry or niche. By developing a strategic content marketing plan, leveraging unique expertise, consistently creating valuable content, and actively engaging with the target audience and industry peers, brands can differentiate themselves, build trust and credibility, and foster long-term relationships with their audiences.

Thought leadership not only helps to attract and retain customers but also contributes to the overall growth and success of the brand.

* * *

29

The Law of Public Relations

In the realm of brand communication, The Law of Public Relations emphasizes the importance of managing a brand's reputation and relationships with its various stakeholders. Public Relations (PR) encompasses a wide range of strategic communication efforts aimed at shaping public perception, building trust, and fostering positive relationships between a brand and its audiences.

The Law of Public Relations recognizes that a brand's success is heavily influenced by how it is perceived by the public. A positive reputation can lead to increased brand loyalty, customer trust, and business growth, while a negative reputation can have severe consequences, such as loss of customers, decreased sales, and damage to the brand's long-term viability.

To effectively implement The Law of Public Relations, brands must develop a comprehensive PR strategy that aligns with their overall brand identity, values, and goals. This strategy should encompass various aspects of communication, including media relations, crisis management, thought leadership, corporate social responsibility, and stakeholder engagement.

One key aspect of PR is media relations. Brands must proactively engage with journalists, bloggers, and influencers to secure positive media coverage and shape the narrative around their brand. This involves crafting compelling press releases, pitching story ideas, and providing subject matter experts for interviews. By establishing strong relationships with the media, brands can gain valuable third-party endorsements and increase their visibility among target audiences.

Crisis management is another critical component of PR. In today's fast-paced, digital world, brands must be prepared to respond quickly and effectively to potential crises or negative situations that could harm their reputation. This requires having a well-defined crisis communication plan in place, which outlines roles and responsibilities, key messaging, and protocols for addressing various scenarios. By proactively managing crises, brands can minimize damage to their reputation and maintain public trust.

Thought leadership is also an important aspect of PR. By positioning themselves as industry experts and thought leaders, brands can build credibility, trust, and authority among their target audiences. This involves creating and sharing valuable content, such as blog posts, whitepapers, and speaking engagements, that demonstrate the brand's expertise and insights. By establishing themselves as go-to resources in their industries, brands can attract new customers and foster loyalty among existing ones.

Corporate social responsibility (CSR) has become increasingly important in PR. Consumers today expect brands to take a stand on social and environmental issues and make a positive impact on the world. By aligning themselves with causes that matter to their target audiences and actively contributing to social and environmental initiatives, brands can enhance their reputation and build goodwill among stakeholders.

Stakeholder engagement is another key aspect of PR. Brands must actively engage with their various stakeholders, including customers, employees, investors, suppliers, and local communities, to build strong, mutually beneficial relationships. This involves regular communication, transparency, and responsiveness to stakeholder concerns and feedback. By fostering open and honest dialogue with stakeholders, brands can build trust, loyalty, and advocacy.

For example, Patagonia, the outdoor clothing and gear company, is known for its strong commitment to environmental sustainability and activism. Through its PR efforts, Patagonia has positioned itself as a leader in corporate social responsibility, regularly engaging in environmental campaigns, donating a portion of its profits to environmental causes, and using its platform to raise awareness about climate change. By aligning its PR strategy with its core values, Patagonia has built a loyal customer base and a reputation as a purpose-driven brand.

Another example is Airbnb, which faced a significant PR challenge in 2020 due to the impact of the COVID-19 pandemic on the travel industry. Airbnb quickly adapted its PR strategy to focus on supporting its hosts and communities, launching initiatives such as the Superhost Relief Fund and the Frontline Stays program, which provided free housing to healthcare workers and first responders. By prioritizing stakeholder engagement and social responsibility during a crisis, Airbnb was able to maintain its reputation and build goodwill among its stakeholders.

In conclusion, The Law of Public Relations underscores the vital role that strategic communication plays in managing a brand's reputation and relationships with its stakeholders. By developing a comprehensive PR strategy that encompasses media relations, crisis management, thought leadership, corporate social responsibility, and stakeholder engagement, brands can build trust, credibility, and loyalty among their target audiences. Effective PR not only helps protect a brand's reputation but also contributes to its long-term success and growth.

* * *

30

The Law of Social Media

The Law of Social Media is an essential aspect of modern brand communication. In today's digital age, social media platforms have become powerful tools for brands to connect with their target audiences, build relationships, and promote their products or services.

1. **Choose the Right Platforms:** Not all social media platforms are equally relevant for every brand. It's essential to identify the platforms where your target audience is most active and engaged. For example, a B2B company may find LinkedIn more effective for their communication, while a fashion brand may focus on Instagram and Pinterest. By selecting the right platforms, brands can ensure that their message reaches the intended audience.
2. **Develop a Consistent Brand Voice:** Maintaining a consistent brand voice across all social media channels is crucial for building a strong brand identity. This includes the tone, language, and visual elements used in your posts. A consistent brand voice helps your audience recognize and connect with your brand, fostering trust and loyalty.
3. **Create Engaging Content:** Social media is all about engagement. To capture your audience's attention, create content that is informative, entertaining, and valuable. This can include a mix of text, images, videos, and interactive elements such as polls and quizzes. Brands should

also consider the specific features and formats of each platform, such as Instagram Stories or Twitter threads, to create platform-specific content.

4. **Foster Two-Way Communication:** Social media provides an opportunity for brands to have direct conversations with their audience. Encourage your followers to comment, ask questions, and share their opinions. Respond to their inquiries and feedback in a timely and authentic manner. This two-way communication helps build stronger relationships and shows that your brand values its customers' input.

5. **Leverage User-Generated Content:** User-generated content (UGC) is a powerful tool for building credibility and trust. Encourage your customers to share their experiences with your brand on social media, and showcase their content on your own channels. This not only provides social proof but also creates a sense of community around your brand.

6. **Collaborate with Influencers:** Influencer marketing has become a significant aspect of social media communication. Partnering with relevant influencers can help expand your brand's reach and tap into new audiences. However, it's essential to choose influencers who align with your brand values and have a genuine connection with their followers.

7. **Utilize Paid Advertising:** While organic reach on social media has become increasingly challenging, paid advertising offers targeted opportunities to reach your desired audience. Platforms like Facebook, Instagram, and LinkedIn provide sophisticated targeting options based on demographics, interests, and behaviors. By investing in paid advertising, brands can amplify their message and drive specific actions, such as website visits or product purchases.

8. **Monitor and Analyze Performance:** To optimize your social media efforts, it's crucial to regularly monitor and analyze your performance. Most social media platforms provide built-in analytics tools that offer insights into your posts' reach, engagement, and audience demographics. Use this data to identify what types of content resonate with your audience and adjust your strategy accordingly.

Successful Examples:

1. **Wendy's Twitter:** Wendy's, the fast-food chain, has gained a reputation for its witty and sassy Twitter presence. By engaging in humorous exchanges with competitors and fans alike, Wendy's has built a strong brand personality and fostered a loyal following on the platform.
2. **Glossier's Instagram:** Glossier, a beauty brand, has leveraged Instagram to build a highly engaged community. By showcasing user-generated content, providing behind-the-scenes glimpses, and actively engaging with their followers, Glossier has cultivated a strong brand identity and loyal customer base.
3. **Airbnb's Facebook:** Airbnb uses Facebook to inspire travel and showcase unique accommodations. By sharing user stories, travel tips, and stunning visuals, Airbnb creates a sense of wanderlust and community among its followers.

By following The Law of Social Media, brands can effectively leverage these platforms to build relationships, promote their offerings, and drive meaningful engagement with their target audiences. As social media continues to evolve, brands must stay adaptable and attuned to their audience's preferences to maintain a strong and impactful presence.

* * *

31

The Law of Listening

The Law of Listening is a crucial principle in effective brand communication. It emphasizes the importance of actively listening to your target audience, understanding their needs, preferences, and feedback, and adapting your communication strategies accordingly. In today's fast-paced and highly competitive market, brands that genuinely listen to their customers and respond to their concerns are more likely to build strong, lasting relationships and foster brand loyalty.

1. **Monitor Social Media:** Social media platforms provide a wealth of information about your target audience. By monitoring social media conversations, brands can gain valuable insights into their customers' opinions, preferences, and pain points. Tools like Hootsuite, Sprout Social, and Mention can help brands track mentions of their brand name, products, or relevant keywords across various platforms.
2. **Conduct Surveys and Polls:** Surveys and polls are effective ways to gather direct feedback from your audience. They can help brands understand their customers' satisfaction levels, preferences, and areas for improvement. Platforms like SurveyMonkey, Google Forms, and Typeform make it easy to create and distribute surveys to your target audience.
3. **Analyze Customer Feedback:** Brands should actively encourage cus-

tomers to provide feedback through various channels, such as email, customer support, or reviews. By analyzing this feedback, brands can identify common themes, concerns, and opportunities for improvement. This information can be used to refine products, services, and communication strategies to better meet customer needs.

4. **Engage in Active Listening:** Active listening goes beyond simply hearing what your customers are saying. It involves fully concentrating on their message, understanding their perspective, and responding empathetically. When engaging with customers on social media, email, or customer support, brands should practice active listening to build trust and show that they value their customers' opinions.

5. **Respond to Feedback:** Listening to feedback is only the first step; brands must also take action based on what they hear. This may involve making changes to products or services, addressing customer concerns, or adapting communication strategies. By demonstrating that they are responsive to feedback, brands can show their customers that they are valued and heard.

6. **Personalized Communication:** Listening to individual customers' preferences and needs allows brands to personalize their communication. This can involve tailoring email campaigns, product recommendations, or social media interactions based on a customer's past purchases, interests, or behaviour. Personalized communication helps build stronger, more meaningful connections with customers.

7. **Foster a Listening Culture:** To effectively implement The Law of Listening, brands must foster a culture of listening throughout their organization. This involves training employees at all levels to actively listen to customers, share feedback, and collaborate to address concerns. By making listening a core value, brands can ensure that customer needs are consistently prioritized.

Examples:

1. **Starbucks' My Starbucks Idea:** Starbucks launched a platform called

My Starbucks Idea, where customers could submit suggestions, vote on ideas, and engage in discussions. By actively listening to and implementing customer ideas, Starbucks has introduced popular offerings like the Frappuccino and free Wi-Fi in its stores.
2. **Nike's Consumer Insights:** Nike uses a variety of methods, including social media monitoring, surveys, and focus groups, to gather consumer insights. By listening to feedback, Nike has been able to develop innovative products that meet the evolving needs of athletes and fitness enthusiasts.
3. **Airbnb's Host Listening:** Airbnb actively listens to its host community through forums, events, and surveys. By understanding hosts' needs and concerns, Airbnb has introduced features like Host Guarantee insurance and Instant Book to improve the hosting experience.

By embracing The Law of Listening, brands can gain valuable insights, build stronger relationships with their customers, and adapt their strategies to meet evolving needs and preferences. In today's customer-centric market, active listening is no longer optional; it is a critical component of successful brand communication and long-term growth.

* * *

32

The Law of Authenticity(Communication)

The Law of Authenticity is a fundamental principle in modern brand communication. In an era where consumers are increasingly skeptical of advertising and marketing messages, brands that communicate with authenticity and transparency are more likely to build trust, credibility, and long-lasting relationships with their target audience.

1. **Be True to Your Brand Values:** Authenticity in communication starts with having a clear understanding of your brand's core values and mission. These values should guide all aspects of your communication, from the language you use to the stories you tell. By consistently communicating in a way that aligns with your brand values, you can build a strong brand identity and establish trust with your audience.
2. **Embrace Transparency:** Transparency is a key component of authentic communication. Brands should be open and honest about their products, services, and business practices. This includes being upfront about pricing, sourcing, and any potential limitations or challenges. By embracing transparency, brands can demonstrate their integrity and build credibility with their audience.
3. **Show Your Human Side:** Authentic communication often involves showing the human side of your brand. This can include sharing behind-the-scenes content, highlighting employee stories, or using

a conversational tone in your messaging. By showcasing the people and personalities behind your brand, you can create a more relatable and engaging presence that resonates with your audience.

4. **Own Your Mistakes:** No brand is perfect, and mistakes are inevitable. When faced with a challenge or crisis, authentic brands own their mistakes and take responsibility for their actions. They communicate openly and honestly about what went wrong, apologize sincerely, and outline the steps they are taking to make things right. By demonstrating accountability and a commitment to improvement, brands can maintain trust and credibility even in difficult situations.

5. **Engage in Authentic Storytelling:** Authentic storytelling is a powerful way to connect with your audience on an emotional level. Share stories that highlight your brand's purpose, values, and impact. These can include customer success stories, employee spotlights, or initiatives that demonstrate your brand's commitment to social responsibility. Authentic stories help humanize your brand and create a deeper connection with your audience.

6. **Avoid Jumping on Trends:** While it can be tempting to jump on the latest social media trends or viral challenges, authentic brands are selective about the trends they participate in. They focus on trends that align with their brand values and messaging, rather than simply trying to capitalize on popular hashtags or memes. By staying true to your brand's voice and purpose, you can avoid coming across as inauthentic or opportunistic.

7. **Collaborate with Authentic Influencers:** When partnering with influencers or brand ambassadors, it's essential to choose individuals who genuinely align with your brand values and messaging. Authentic influencer collaborations involve working with individuals who have a genuine connection to your brand and can communicate about your products or services in a way that feels natural and credible to their followers.

Examples:

1. **Patagonia's Activism:** Patagonia is known for its authentic commitment to environmental activism. The brand consistently communicates about its sustainability initiatives, advocates for environmental causes, and even encourages customers to buy less and repair their clothing. By aligning its communication with its core values, Patagonia has built a strong reputation for authenticity and integrity.
2. **Dove's Real Beauty Campaign:** Dove's Real Beauty campaign is a powerful example of authentic communication. By featuring real women of diverse ages, sizes, and ethnicities in its advertising, Dove challenged traditional beauty standards and promoted a more inclusive and authentic vision of beauty. The campaign resonated deeply with consumers and helped establish Dove as a brand committed to authenticity and body positivity.
3. **Buffer's Transparency:** Buffer, a social media management platform, is known for its transparent communication. The company openly shares its revenue, salaries, and even its challenges and failures with its audience. By embracing radical transparency, Buffer has built a strong reputation for authenticity and trust within its industry.

By embracing The Law of Authenticity, brands can build stronger, more meaningful connections with their target audience. Authentic communication involves staying true to your brand values, embracing transparency, showing your human side, owning your mistakes, engaging in authentic storytelling, avoiding inauthentic trend-jumping, and collaborating with genuine influencers. By prioritizing authenticity in all aspects of their communication, brands can differentiate themselves in a crowded market and build lasting relationships with their customers.

***

VI

Part 06—Brand Evolution

33

The Law of Extension

In today's fast-paced and ever-evolving business landscape, building a great brand requires more than just establishing a strong presence in a single market or product category. To achieve long-term success and sustainability, brands must be designed with extensibility in mind from the very beginning. The Law of Extension emphasizes the importance of creating a brand that is capable of expanding into different categories, diversifying its reach, and tapping into new markets, all while staying true to its core values and identity.

1. **Designing for Extensibility:** When building a brand, it is crucial to lay a foundation that allows for future growth and diversification. This means defining the brand's core values, purpose, and personality in a way that is broad enough to accommodate expansion into new territories yet specific enough to maintain a clear and consistent identity. Brands should avoid defining themselves too narrowly in terms of product categories or target audiences, as this can limit their ability to extend into new areas when opportunities arise.
2. **Identifying Extensible Brand Elements:** To create an extensible brand, companies must identify the key elements of their brand that can be leveraged across different categories and markets. These elements may include the brand's core values, unique selling proposition, visual

identity, and brand personality. By ensuring that these elements are flexible and adaptable, brands can maintain consistency and recognition as they expand into new areas. For example, a brand known for its commitment to sustainability can extend this value into different product categories, such as fashion, beauty, or home goods, while maintaining a cohesive brand narrative.

3. **Conducting Market Research and Analysis:** Before extending a brand into new categories or markets, it is essential to conduct thorough market research and analysis. This involves identifying potential opportunities, assessing consumer needs and preferences, and evaluating the competitive landscape. By gathering insights and data, brands can make informed decisions about where to expand and how to position themselves in new markets. This research should also consider the brand's existing strengths and resources, as well as any potential risks or challenges associated with the extension.

4. **Developing a Strategic Extension Plan:** Once potential extension opportunities have been identified, brands must develop a strategic plan to guide their expansion efforts. This plan should outline the specific goals and objectives of the extension, as well as the tactics and resources required to achieve them. It should also consider the potential impact of the extension on the brand's existing offerings and customer base, as well as any necessary adjustments to the brand's messaging and communication strategies. A well-crafted extension plan will help ensure a smooth and successful transition into new markets while maintaining the brand's integrity and core identity.

5. **Engaging Customers and Building Loyalty:** As brands extend into new categories and markets, it is crucial to engage customers and build loyalty. This involves communicating the brand's values and unique propositions consistently across all touchpoints and delivering on the brand's promises. Brands should also seek to create emotional connections with customers by understanding their needs, preferences, and aspirations, and by providing experiences that resonate with them on a personal level. By fostering strong relationships with customers,

brands can create a loyal following that will support them as they expand into new areas.

6. **Monitoring and Adapting to Market Dynamics:** The success of a brand extension depends not only on the initial strategy and execution but also on the ability to monitor and adapt to changing market dynamics. Brands must continuously track the performance of their extensions, gather customer feedback, and stay attuned to emerging trends and competitive threats. By being agile and responsive, brands can make necessary adjustments to their extension strategies, optimize their offerings, and capitalize on new opportunities as they arise.

Building a great brand requires a long-term vision and a commitment to extensibility from the outset. By designing for extensibility, identifying extensible brand elements, conducting market research, developing a strategic extension plan, engaging customers, and monitoring market dynamics, brands can successfully extend into new categories and markets while staying true to their core values. The Law of Extension is a critical component of brand evolution, enabling brands to grow, adapt, and thrive in an ever-changing business landscape.

Virgin

Virgin, a multinational venture capital conglomerate, stands as a shining example of how a brand can successfully apply the Law of Extension to build a diverse and resilient portfolio. From its humble beginnings as a mail-order record retailer in 1970, Virgin has grown into a global powerhouse, with a presence in industries ranging from travel and entertainment to healthcare and space tourism.

The key to Virgin's success lies in its founder, Sir Richard Branson's, vision for the brand. From the outset, Branson designed Virgin with extensibility in mind, creating a brand that stood for quality, innovation, and customer-centricity – values that could be applied across a wide range of industries. By defining the brand's core purpose as "changing business for good" and its personality as "fun, irreverent, and adventurous," Virgin laid the foundation for future extensions into diverse sectors.

As Virgin grew, it consistently leveraged its core brand elements to extend into new categories. The brand's signature red colour, cheeky tone of voice, and focus on customer experience have been applied across a wide range of businesses, from Virgin Atlantic in the airline industry to Virgin Mobile in telecommunications and even Virgin Galactic in space tourism. By maintaining these consistent brand elements, Virgin has been able to establish instant recognition and credibility in new markets, even when entering highly competitive industries.

However, Virgin's success is not solely attributed to its brand identity. The company conducts extensive market research and analysis before extending into new categories, identifying opportunities that align with its brand values and competencies. For example, before launching Virgin America in 2004, the company identified a gap in the U.S. airline market for a high-quality, customer-focused carrier that could disrupt the status quo. By analyzing consumer preferences, competitive dynamics, and regulatory requirements, Virgin was able to develop a differentiated offering that resonated with customers and quickly gained market share.

Once Virgin identifies a new opportunity, it develops a strategic plan that outlines the key goals, target audiences, and competitive positioning of the new venture, as well as the resources and partnerships required for success. This strategic approach ensures that each extension aligns with the brand's core values and objectives, such as the potential for innovation, the ability to deliver superior customer experiences, and the opportunity to make a positive impact on society and the environment.

One of Virgin's greatest strengths is its ability to engage customers and build loyalty across all of its businesses. The brand is renowned for its exceptional customer service, personalized experiences, and innovative loyalty programs. Virgin Atlantic's "Flying Club" rewards program, for instance, offers unique benefits such as access to exclusive events and experiences, while Virgin Mobile's "Virgin Red" app provides customers with personalized offers and rewards based on their interests and behavior. By consistently delivering on its brand promise and creating emotional connections with customers, Virgin has cultivated a loyal following that spans multiple industries.

As Virgin has extended into new categories, it has continually monitored market trends and adapted its strategies accordingly. In the face of the COVID-19 pandemic, Virgin Atlantic pivoted its business model to focus on cargo operations and virtual experiences, while Virgin Galactic adjusted its timeline for commercial space flights. By being agile and responsive to changing market conditions, Virgin has been able to navigate challenges and identify new opportunities for growth.

Virgin's successful application of the Law of Extension serves as a valuable guide for brands seeking to build a diverse and resilient portfolio. By designing for extensibility, leveraging core brand elements, conducting thorough market research, developing strategic extension plans, engaging customers, and adapting to market dynamics, Virgin has been able to extend its brand into a wide range of industries while maintaining a consistent and compelling brand identity. As a result, Virgin has become one of the most recognizable and respected brands in the world, with a reputation for innovation, customer-centricity, and positive impact.

* * *

34

The Law of Evolution

In the ever-changing landscape of business, brands that remain static risk becoming irrelevant and losing their competitive edge. The Law of Evolution emphasizes the importance of continuous adaptation and transformation to ensure long-term success and sustainability. This law encourages brands to embrace change, anticipate future trends, and proactively evolve to meet the shifting needs and expectations of their customers.

One brand that exemplifies the Law of Evolution is Amazon, the global e-commerce giant. Founded in 1994 as an online bookstore, Amazon has continuously evolved its business model and expanded its offerings to stay ahead of the curve and maintain its position as a market leader.

In its early days, Amazon recognized the potential of the internet to revolutionize the way people shop. By offering a wide selection of books at competitive prices and delivering them directly to customers' doorsteps, Amazon quickly gained traction and established itself as a pioneer in e-commerce. However, the company's founder, Jeff Bezos, knew that to sustain growth and remain relevant, Amazon would need to evolve beyond books.

As the internet became more ubiquitous and customer preferences shifted, Amazon began to expand its product categories. The company started selling music, movies, and video games, before eventually branching out into electronics, toys, and home goods. By continuously adding new product lines and improving its online shopping experience, Amazon was able to attract a broader customer base and establish itself as a one-stop-shop for online retail.

But Amazon's evolution didn't stop there. The company recognized the growing importance of technology and innovation in driving business success. In 2006, Amazon launched Amazon Web Services (AWS), a cloud computing platform that would revolutionize the way businesses build and deploy applications. AWS quickly became a major player in the cloud computing market, providing a new revenue stream for Amazon and solidifying its position as a technology leader.

Amazon's evolution also extended to its business model. In addition to its e-commerce platform, the company launched Amazon Prime, a subscription service that offers customers free shipping, streaming video and music, and other exclusive benefits. By creating a loyalty program that provides tangible value to customers, Amazon was able to drive repeat business and increase customer lifetime value.

As Amazon continued to evolve, it also recognized the importance of expanding into new markets and industries. The company acquired Whole Foods Market in 2017, signaling its entry into the grocery and brick-and-mortar retail space. This move allowed Amazon to combine its expertise in e-commerce and logistics with Whole Foods' strong brand reputation and physical store presence, creating a powerful omnichannel retail experience.

Throughout its history, Amazon has demonstrated a remarkable ability to anticipate and respond to changing market conditions and customer needs. By continually evolving its business model, expanding its offerings, and embracing new technologies and innovations, Amazon has been able to stay ahead of the curve and maintain its position as a market leader.

Amazon's success story serves as a valuable lesson for brands seeking to apply the Law of Evolution. To thrive in today's fast-paced and ever-changing business environment, brands must be willing to adapt and transform. This requires a deep understanding of customer needs and preferences, as well as a keen awareness of emerging trends and technologies.

Brands that embrace the Law of Evolution are better positioned to identify new growth opportunities, enter new markets, and create innovative products and services that meet the evolving needs of their customers. By fostering a culture of continuous learning, experimentation, and adaptation, brands can stay relevant and competitive in the face of change.

Netflix

Netflix is an excellent example of a brand that has successfully evolved over time, adapting to changing market conditions, consumer preferences, and technological advancements. From its humble beginnings as a DVD-by-mail rental service to its current position as a global streaming giant and content creator, Netflix has consistently demonstrated the power of brand evolution.

1. **DVD Rental Origins (1997-2007):** Netflix was founded in 1997 as a DVD-by-mail rental service, offering customers a wide selection of movies and TV shows delivered directly to their doorstep. At the time, the company's main competitor was Blockbuster, which dominated the video rental market with its brick-and-mortar stores. Netflix differentiated itself by offering a subscription-based model with no late fees, a more convenient rental process, and a broader selection of titles.
2. **Transition to Streaming (2007-2012):** As internet speeds improved and streaming technology advanced, Netflix recognized the potential for a new way to consume entertainment. In 2007, the company launched its streaming service, allowing subscribers to watch movies and TV shows instantly on their computers. This move marked a significant shift in Netflix's business model and set the stage for its future growth and evolution.
3. **International Expansion (2010-2016):** With its streaming service gaining popularity in the United States, Netflix began to expand internationally, first to Canada in 2010, followed by Latin America and the Caribbean in 2011. The company continued its global expansion over the

next several years, launching in Europe, Asia, and Australia. By 2016, Netflix was available in over 190 countries, cementing its position as a global streaming leader.

4. **Original Content Creation (2013-Present):** As competition in the streaming market intensified, with the entry of players like Amazon Prime Video and Hulu, Netflix recognized the need to differentiate itself through exclusive content. In 2013, the company released its first original series, "House of Cards," which became a critical and commercial success. Since then, Netflix has invested heavily in original content creation, producing a wide range of movies, TV shows, documentaries, and stand-up specials.

5. **Personalization and Algorithmic Recommendations (2000s-Present):** Throughout its evolution, Netflix has placed a strong emphasis on personalization and using data to enhance the user experience. The company's sophisticated recommendation algorithm, which suggests content based on a user's viewing history and preferences, has been a key driver of engagement and retention. Netflix has continuously refined its algorithm over the years, leveraging advances in machine learning and artificial intelligence to deliver highly personalized viewing experiences.

6. **Mobile and Interactive Content (2010s-Present):** As smartphones and tablets became ubiquitous, Netflix adapted its platform to ensure a seamless mobile viewing experience. The company has also experimented with new forms of interactive content, such as "Black Mirror: Bandersnatch," which allows viewers to make choices that affect the story's outcome. These innovations demonstrate Netflix's willingness to evolve and push the boundaries of traditional entertainment formats.

7. **Brand Partnerships and Merchandise (2010s-Present):** Netflix has also evolved its brand through strategic partnerships and merchandise offerings. The company has collaborated with major brands like Nike, Coca-Cola, and Ben & Jerry's to create co-branded products and experiences tied to its original content. Netflix has also launched its own line of merchandise, including apparel, accessories, and collectibles, further extending its brand presence and engagement with fans.

Throughout its evolution, Netflix has remained true to its core value proposition of providing convenient, affordable access to a wide variety of entertainment content. By continually adapting to changing market conditions, consumer preferences, and technological advancements, Netflix has not only survived but thrived in an increasingly competitive and dynamic industry.

Netflix's journey serves as a powerful case study for the Law of Evolution, demonstrating how a willingness to adapt, innovate, and take risks can help a brand stay relevant and successful over the long term.

Strategies for Brand Evolution

When it comes to applying the Law of Evolution to your own brand, there are several key strategies and principles to keep in mind. Here are some actionable steps and best practices for ensuring that your brand remains relevant, competitive, and profitable in an ever-changing business landscape:

1. **Stay customer-centric:** The most successful brands are those that prioritize the needs and preferences of their customers. Make sure to regularly gather customer feedback, monitor changing trends and behaviors, and use these insights to guide your brand's evolution. By staying attuned to your customers' evolving needs and expectations, you can adapt your offerings and positioning in ways that keep them engaged and loyal.
2. **Embrace data and technology:** In today's digital age, data and technology are essential tools for driving brand evolution. Invest in analytics and machine learning capabilities to better understand your customers, optimize your offerings, and personalize your marketing and communications. Leverage emerging technologies like artificial intelligence, augmented reality, and blockchain to create new and innovative experiences that set your brand apart.
3. **Foster a culture of innovation:** To stay ahead of the curve, your brand needs to cultivate a culture that encourages experimentation,

risk-taking, and continuous learning. Empower your teams to think creatively, test new ideas, and learn from failures. Celebrate successes and share best practices across the organization to drive ongoing innovation and improvement.

4. **Expand into new markets and verticals:** One of the keys to sustained growth and evolution is expanding into new markets and business areas. Conduct thorough market research to identify untapped opportunities, and develop a clear strategy for entering and competing in these new spaces. Consider partnerships, acquisitions, or organic growth as potential paths to expansion, depending on your brand's resources and capabilities.

5. **Adapt your business model:** As your brand evolves, you may need to adapt your business model to better align with changing market conditions and customer needs. This could involve shifting from a product-based to a service-based model, adopting a subscription or recurring revenue approach, or exploring new pricing and distribution strategies. Be open to pivoting your business model when necessary to stay competitive and profitable.

6. **Invest in talent and capabilities:** To drive ongoing evolution and growth, your brand needs the right talent and capabilities in place. Invest in recruiting, developing, and retaining top talent across key functions like marketing, product development, and data analytics. Provide ongoing training and development opportunities to keep your teams' skills and knowledge up-to-date, and foster a diverse and inclusive workplace that encourages different perspectives and ideas.

7. **Measure and iterate:** Finally, to ensure that your brand's evolution is on track and delivering results, it's important to establish clear metrics and regularly measure progress. Set specific, measurable goals for key performance indicators like customer acquisition, engagement, and loyalty, and track these metrics over time. Use these insights to continuously iterate and optimize your strategies, making data-driven decisions that keep your brand moving forward.

When it comes to applying the Law of Evolution to your brand, another crucial aspect is to stay ahead of the curve by tracking emerging trends, changing user attitudes, and new technologies. This proactive approach allows you to anticipate shifts in the market and adapt your brand accordingly, ensuring that you remain relevant and competitive in the long run.

Here are some key strategies for tracking these important factors and incorporating them into your brand evolution:

1. **Monitor emerging trends:** Keep a close eye on emerging trends in your industry and adjacent sectors. This could include new consumer behaviors, shifts in preferences, or changes in the competitive landscape. Attend industry conferences, read trade publications, and follow thought leaders on social media to stay informed. By identifying and capitalizing on emerging trends early, you can position your brand as a leader and innovator in your space.

2. **Understand changing user attitudes:** User attitudes and preferences can shift rapidly, especially in today's fast-paced digital landscape. Regularly conduct market research and gather customer feedback to understand how your target audience's needs, values, and expectations are evolving. Use tools like social media listening, surveys, and focus groups to gain insights into changing user attitudes, and adapt your brand messaging and offerings accordingly.

3. **Explore emerging technologies:** New technologies are constantly emerging, and they have the potential to disrupt entire industries and transform the way brands interact with customers. Stay informed about emerging technologies like artificial intelligence, augmented reality, blockchain, and the Internet of Things, and explore how they could be applied to your brand. Consider partnering with technology companies or investing in R&D to stay at the forefront of technological innovation.

4. **Observe next-generation customers:** The younger generation, including Gen Z and beyond, represents the future of your customer base. Make sure to observe and understand their unique preferences, behaviours, and values, as they may differ significantly from those of previous

generations. Engage with next-generation customers through social media, influencer partnerships, and targeted marketing campaigns, and adapt your brand messaging and offerings to resonate with their evolving needs and expectations.

5. **Pay attention to extremes and outliers:** Sometimes, the most valuable insights for brand evolution come from observing the extremes and outliers in your customer base. These could be your most passionate brand advocates, your most vocal critics, or customers with unique needs or preferences. By understanding what drives these extremes and outliers, you can identify emerging trends and opportunities for innovation that could eventually become mainstream.

Once you have tracked these important factors, the next step is to incorporate them into your brand evolution strategy.

Remember, brand evolution is not a one-time event, but an ongoing process that requires continuous monitoring, iteration, and adaptation. By making tracking and incorporating these important factors a core part of your brand strategy, you can build a brand that not only survives but thrives in the face of change and uncertainty.

* * *

35

The Law of Agility

In today's fast-paced, ever-changing business landscape, the ability to adapt quickly and effectively is more critical than ever. This is where the Law of Agility comes into play. This law states that brands must be nimble, responsive, and able to rapidly pivot in the face of new challenges and opportunities. Agility is not just about speed; it's about the ability to anticipate change, make informed decisions quickly, and execute strategies with precision and flexibility.

The Importance of Agility

Agility is essential for several reasons. First, consumer preferences and behaviours are changing at an unprecedented rate. What may have been relevant and appealing to customers yesterday may not be so today. Brands that can't keep up with these changes risk losing relevance and market share to more nimble competitors.

Second, the competitive landscape is more dynamic than ever. New players can emerge seemingly overnight, disrupting entire industries with innovative business models and technologies. Established brands that are slow to respond to these threats may find themselves quickly outpaced and outmaneuvered.

Finally, in an interconnected global economy, events and disruptions in one part of the world can have rapid and far-reaching consequences for brands everywhere. Whether it's a natural disaster, a political upheaval, or a public health crisis, brands that can adapt quickly to these changing circumstances are better positioned to mitigate risks and seize new opportunities.

Characteristics of Agile Brands

So, what does agility look like in practice? Agile brands tend to share several key characteristics:

1. **Flat hierarchies and decentralized decision-making:** Agile brands have streamlined organizational structures that allow for rapid decision-making and execution. They empower frontline employees and teams to make decisions and take action without getting bogged down in bureaucracy or red tape.
2. **Iterative and experimental processes:** Agile brands embrace a culture of experimentation and continuous improvement. They launch new initiatives quickly, gather feedback, and iterate based on what they learn. They're not afraid to fail fast and pivot when necessary.
3. **Data-driven insights:** Agile brands leverage data and analytics to inform their strategies and decision-making. They continuously monitor key metrics and use real-time insights to adapt their approaches on the fly.
4. **Cross-functional collaboration:** Agile brands break down silos and foster collaboration across functions and departments. They recognize that the best ideas and solutions often emerge from the intersection of diverse perspectives and skill sets.
5. **Flexibility and adaptability:** Agile brands are built for change. They have flexible processes, systems, and mindsets that allow them to quickly pivot in response to new challenges and opportunities.

Strategies for Cultivating Agility

Becoming an agile brand doesn't happen overnight. It requires a deliberate and sustained effort to cultivate the right mindset, processes, and capabilities. Here are some strategies that brands can use to become more agile:

1. **Foster a culture of agility:** Agility starts with culture. Leaders must model and reward behaviors that promote flexibility, experimentation, and continuous learning. They must create an environment where it's safe to take risks and fail fast.
2. **Invest in agile methodologies and processes:** Brands can adopt agile methodologies like Scrum or Kanban to streamline their processes and improve their speed and responsiveness. These approaches emphasize iterative development, cross-functional collaboration, and continuous feedback and improvement.
3. **Empower frontline teams:** Agile brands decentralize decision-making and empower frontline teams to take action. This requires investing in training and development to ensure that employees have the skills and knowledge they need to make informed decisions.
4. **Leverage technology and data:** Technology and data are critical enablers of agility. Brands should invest in tools and platforms that provide real-time insights and enable rapid experimentation and iteration. They should also develop the analytical capabilities needed to turn data into actionable insights.
5. **Embrace partnerships and ecosystems:** No brand can be agile on its own. Agile brands cultivate partnerships and participate in ecosystems that allow them to tap into new sources of innovation, expertise, and agility. They collaborate with startups, academia, and even competitors to stay at the forefront of change.

Examples of Agile Brands

There are many examples of brands that have successfully cultivated agility and used it to their advantage. Here are a few:

1. **Zara:** The Spanish fast-fashion retailer is renowned for its agility. It can design, produce, and deliver new styles to stores in a matter of weeks, allowing it to quickly respond to changing fashion trends and customer preferences.
2. **Netflix:** The streaming giant has disrupted the entertainment industry with its agility. It has leveraged data and analytics to rapidly develop and launch new content, and has continuously evolved its business model in response to changing market conditions.
3. **Amazon:** Amazon's agility is legendary. The company has continuously expanded into new markets and categories, from e-commerce to cloud computing to healthcare. It has also pioneered agile methodologies like "two-pizza teams" to foster rapid innovation and experimentation.
4. **Airbnb:** The home-sharing platform has demonstrated remarkable agility in the face of the COVID-19 pandemic. It quickly pivoted to focus on longer-term stays and local travel and launched new offerings like online experiences to adapt to changing consumer behaviours.

The Law of Agility is a critical principle for brands seeking to thrive in today's fast-paced and unpredictable business landscape. By cultivating the mindset, processes, and capabilities needed for agility, brands can better anticipate and respond to change, and seize new opportunities for growth and innovation. While becoming an agile brand is not easy, the rewards – in terms of increased resilience, competitiveness, and customer loyalty – are well worth the effort.

* * *

36

The Law of Innovation

In an era of rapid change and intense competition, brands that fail to innovate risk falling behind and becoming irrelevant. The Law of Innovation states that brands must continually seek out new ways to create value for their customers and differentiate themselves from competitors. This involves not just developing new products and services, but also reimagining business models, customer experiences, and even entire industries.

The Imperative for Innovation Innovation is no longer optional for brands – it's a necessity. Several factors are driving this imperative:

1. **Changing customer expectations:** Today's customers expect brands to continually offer new and improved products, services, and experiences. They're looking for brands that can anticipate their needs and solve their problems in novel ways.
2. **Technological disruption:** Advances in technology, from artificial intelligence to blockchain, are enabling entirely new ways of doing business. Brands that don't keep pace with these changes risk being disrupted by more innovative competitors.
3. **Commoditization:** In many industries, traditional sources of differentiation, like price or quality, are no longer enough to stand out. Brands need to innovate to create new sources of value and differentiation.

4. **Globalization:** As markets become more global and interconnected, brands face increased competition from players around the world. Innovation is key to staying ahead of the curve and maintaining a competitive edge.

Types of Innovation

Innovation can take many different forms, depending on a brand's industry, capabilities, and strategic objectives. Some common types of innovation include:

1. **Product innovation:** This involves developing new products or significantly improving existing ones. Product innovation can be driven by new technologies, changing customer needs, or shifts in market trends.
2. **Service innovation:** Service innovation involves creating new or improved services that deliver value to customers in novel ways. This can include everything from new customer support channels to entirely new service models.
3. **Business model innovation:** This involves fundamentally rethinking how a brand creates, delivers, and captures value. Business model innovation can involve changes to pricing, distribution, or even the core offering itself.
4. **Experience innovation:** Experience innovation focuses on creating unique and memorable customer experiences. This can involve everything from personalized interactions to immersive digital environments.
5. **Process innovation:** Process innovation involves finding new and better ways to perform key business processes, from manufacturing to marketing. The goal is to improve efficiency, quality, and speed while reducing costs.

Strategies for Driving Innovation

Cultivating a culture of innovation is key to driving ongoing brand evolution. Here are some strategies that brands can use to embed innovation into their DNA:

1. **Embrace a growth mindset:** Innovative brands cultivate a growth mindset that values learning, experimentation, and continuous improvement. They see challenges as opportunities to learn and grow.
2. **Foster creativity:** Creativity is the fuel for innovation. Brands can foster creativity by encouraging diverse perspectives, providing resources and support for idea generation, and celebrating creative thinking.
3. **Collaborate across boundaries:** Innovation often happens at the intersection of different disciplines, perspectives, and experiences. Brands should break down silos and encourage collaboration across functions, geographies, and even industries.
4. **Engage customers:** Customers are often the best source of insights and ideas for innovation. Brands should actively engage customers in the innovation process, from ideation to co-creation to feedback and testing.
5. **Invest in innovation:** Innovation requires sustained investment, both in terms of financial resources and human capital. Brands should create dedicated innovation budgets and teams, and provide them with the tools, training, and support they need to succeed.
6. **Embrace failure:** Not every innovation will be a success. Innovative brands embrace failure as a necessary part of the learning process. They quickly pivot from failures and apply the lessons learned to future initiatives.

Examples of Innovative Brands

Many of the world's most successful and admired brands are also some of the most innovative. Here are a few examples:

1. **Apple:** Apple has consistently set the standard for innovation in consumer electronics. From the iPod to the iPhone to the Apple Watch, the company has reimagined entire product categories and created entirely new ones.
2. **Tesla:** Tesla has disrupted the automotive industry with its innovative electric vehicles and direct-to-consumer sales model. The company continues to push the boundaries of what's possible with autonomous driving, battery technology, and even solar power.
3. **Airbnb:** Airbnb innovated the travel industry by allowing individuals to rent out their homes to travelers. The company has continued to innovate with offerings like Experiences, which allow travelers to book unique activities led by local hosts.
4. **Warby Parker:** Warby Parker innovated the eyewear industry by offering stylish, affordable glasses online with a try-at-home model. The company has continued to innovate with virtual try-on tools, in-store experiences, and even a line of contact lenses.

The Law of Innovation is a critical principle for brands seeking to stay ahead in a rapidly changing world. By continually seeking out new ways to create value and differentiate themselves, brands can not only survive but thrive in the face of disruption. While innovation requires a significant investment of time, resources, and effort, the payoff – in terms of increased growth, competitiveness, and customer loyalty – is well worth it. As the pace of change continues to accelerate, the brands that will win will be those that make innovation a core part of their DNA and a driving force for ongoing evolution.

* * *

37

The Law of Resilience

In the journey of brand evolution, setbacks and challenges are inevitable. Economic downturns, shifting consumer preferences, technological disruptions, and even global crises can all put immense pressure on brands. However, some brands not only survive these challenges but emerge stronger. This is where the Law of Resilience comes into play. This law states that a brand's ability to bounce back from adversity, adapt to change, and continue growing is directly proportional to its resilience.

Understanding Resilience

Resilience is the capacity to recover quickly from difficulties. For brands, it means having the strength and adaptability to weather storms, learning from setbacks, and continuing to move forward. It's not about avoiding challenges altogether but rather about developing the capabilities and mindset to deal with them effectively when they arise.

Resilient brands share certain characteristics. They have a clear sense of purpose and values that guide them through tough times. They have strong relationships with their customers, built on trust and loyalty. They have agile and adaptable business models that can pivot quickly in response to changing circumstances. And they have a culture of learning and innovation that allows them to continuously evolve and improve.

Building Brand Resilience

Building resilience is a key part of brand evolution. Here are some strategies that brands can use to cultivate resilience:

1. **Develop a strong brand foundation:** A clear brand purpose, values, and identity serve as a solid foundation during times of change. They provide a north star that guides decision-making and keeps the brand true to itself.
2. **Foster customer loyalty:** Strong customer relationships are a key source of resilience. Brands that have earned the trust and loyalty of their customers are better positioned to retain them during challenging times.
3. **Diversify the business:** Brands that rely too heavily on a single product, market, or revenue stream are more vulnerable to disruptions. Diversifying the business across multiple areas helps spread risk and creates more avenues for growth.
4. **Build financial strength:** Having a strong financial position, with ample cash reserves and manageable debt, provides a buffer during economic downturns. It allows brands to continue investing in their business and seizing new opportunities.
5. **Invest in talent and culture:** A resilient workforce is key to a resilient brand. Investing in employee development, fostering a positive culture, and attracting top talent all contribute to an organization's ability to adapt and thrive.
6. **Embrace change and innovation:** Resilient brands don't just react to change, they proactively seek it out. They continuously experiment with new ideas, learn from failures, and evolve their business to stay ahead of the curve.

The Resilience Cycle

Building resilience is not a one-time event but a continuous cycle. The Resilience Cycle involves four key stages:

1. **Prepare:** This stage involves assessing potential risks and challenges, developing contingency plans, and building the capabilities needed to respond effectively.
2. **Absorb:** When a challenge hits, resilient brands are able to absorb the shock. They have the resources, relationships, and mindset to weather the initial impact.
3. **Recover:** In the recovery stage, brands assess the damage, learn from the experience, and begin to bounce back. They adapt their strategies and operations as needed to address new realities.
4. **Grow:** Resilient brands don't just recover from their previous state; they use challenges as springboards for growth. They seize new opportunities, innovate their business, and emerge stronger than before.

Examples of Resilient Brands

Throughout history, there are many examples of brands that have demonstrated remarkable resilience in the face of adversity. Here are a few:

1. **Apple:** In the late 1990s, Apple was on the brink of bankruptcy. But with the return of Steve Jobs and a renewed focus on innovation, the company bounced back and went on to become one of the most valuable brands in the world.
2. **Lego:** In the early 2000s, Lego was facing declining sales and heavy debt. But by refocusing on its core products, investing in innovation, and expanding into new areas like movies and video games, the company staged a remarkable turnaround.
3. **Airbnb:** The COVID-19 pandemic hit Airbnb hard, with travel grinding to a halt worldwide. But the company quickly adapted, pivoting to longer-

term stays, promoting local travel, and cutting costs. As a result, it was able to weather the storm and position itself for growth as travel rebounds.
4. **Starbucks:** In 2008, Starbucks was struggling with over-expansion and a diluted brand. However, by closing underperforming stores, refocusing on the customer experience, and investing in digital innovation, the company was able to bounce back and continue growing.

The Law of Resilience is a critical principle for brands seeking to thrive in an uncertain and ever-changing world. By building the capabilities and mindset needed to bounce back from adversity, adapt to change, and seize new opportunities, brands can not only survive but flourish over the long term. While developing resilience requires ongoing effort and investment, the rewards – in terms of increased strength, adaptability, and growth – are well worth it. In the end, the brands that will stand the test of time will be those that can not only weather storms but emerge from them better and stronger than before.

* * *

Conclusion

Throughout this book, we have explored the fundamental laws that govern the world of branding. From the importance of customer-centricity and defining your brand's strategic foundation to crafting a compelling brand identity, delivering exceptional experiences, communicating effectively, and embracing evolution, these laws provide a comprehensive framework for building and managing successful brands.

However, knowing the laws is just the first step. To truly master the art of branding, you must learn how to apply these laws in a way that is authentic, consistent, and tailored to your unique brand and target audience.

Here are some key pieces of advice to help you put these laws into practice:

1. **Start with your customers:** Always keep your customers at the heart of your branding efforts. Continuously seek to understand their needs, desires, and pain points, and use these insights to inform every aspect of your brand strategy.
2. **Be authentic:** Your brand must be true to its core values and purpose. Don't try to be something you're not, as customers can quickly spot inauthenticity. Embrace your unique strengths and let them shine through in your brand identity and communications.
3. **Consistency is key:** Ensure that your brand is consistently represented across all touchpoints, from your visual identity to your customer experience. Consistency builds trust and reinforces your brand's message in the minds of your customers.
4. **Embrace storytelling:** Use the power of storytelling to connect with your audience on an emotional level. Craft compelling narratives that showcase your brand's personality, values, and purpose, and inspire

CONCLUSION

your customers to become part of your brand story.
5. **Focus on experiences:** In today's competitive landscape, exceptional experiences are what set brands apart. Continuously strive to overdeliver on your brand promise and create memorable, personalized experiences that foster emotional connections and build long-lasting relationships with your customers.
6. **Adapt and evolve:** Brands must be agile and responsive to changes in the market, customer preferences, and technological advancements. Embrace innovation and be willing to evolve your brand strategy when necessary, while staying true to your core values and purpose.

Remember, building a strong brand is an ongoing journey that requires dedication, creativity, and a customer-centric mindset. Embrace the process, stay true to your brand's purpose, and always strive to create meaningful connections with your customers.

The Interconnectedness of the Laws

Many of the laws of branding are interconnected and work together to create a cohesive and effective brand strategy. For example:

- The Law of Customer-Centricity is closely linked to the Law of Value Proposition, as understanding your customers' needs and desires is essential for crafting a compelling value proposition.
- The Law of Consistency applies to both brand identity and brand experience, ensuring that your brand is consistently represented across all touchpoints.
- The Law of Authenticity is relevant to both brand identity and brand communication, as it emphasizes the importance of staying true to your brand's core values and purpose.

Recognizing these interconnections can help you develop a more holistic and integrated approach to branding, ensuring that all aspects of your brand work together seamlessly.

The Overlapping of Laws

There is some overlap among the laws, particularly those under the Brand Experience category. This overlap is not surprising, as many aspects of brand experience are interconnected and work together to create a cohesive and memorable experience for customers.

For instance, the Law of Consistency (Experience) is closely tied to the Law of Holistic Experience Design. To create a consistent brand experience, you must ensure that all touchpoints and interactions with your brand are designed cohesively and align with your brand's identity and values.

Similarly, the Law of Emotional Connection is related to the Law of Personalization and the Law of Building Relationships (With Customers). By personalizing experiences and interactions, brands can forge stronger emotional connections with their customers, which in turn helps build lasting relationships.

The Law of Community also ties into the Law of Building Relationships (With Customers), as fostering a sense of community among your customers can deepen their connection to your brand and strengthen their loyalty.

While these overlaps exist, each law still brings a unique perspective and focus to the overall brand experience. The Law of Experiential Branding, for example, emphasizes the importance of creating immersive and engaging experiences, while the Law of Overdelivering stresses the need to exceed customer expectations consistently.

Recognizing these overlaps can help brand managers and marketers understand the interconnectedness of various aspects of brand experience. By addressing these laws holistically and ensuring that they work together seamlessly, brands can create more compelling, cohesive, and memorable experiences for their customers.

Applicability of the Laws

While the laws of branding provide a comprehensive framework, it's important to recognize that not all laws may be equally applicable to every brand. The relevance and importance of each law may vary depending on factors such as:

1. Target audience: The importance of certain laws may vary based on your target audience's preferences and expectations. For example, the Law of Personalization may be more important for brands targeting younger, digitally-savvy consumers.
2. Brand maturity: The focus of your branding efforts may shift as your brand evolves. For example, the Law of Extension may become more relevant as your brand grows and seeks to expand into new product categories or markets.
3. Resources and capabilities: The extent to which you can apply certain laws may depend on your brand's resources and capabilities. For example, smaller brands may need to be more selective in their application of the Law of Innovation due to limited resources.

When applying the laws of branding, it's essential to consider your brand's unique context and prioritize the laws that are most relevant and impactful for your specific situation. This requires a deep understanding of your brand, your customers, and your market, as well as a willingness to adapt your approach as needed.

* * *

About the Author

Shah Mohammed is an accomplished Business Strategy and design-thinking consultant with a passion for innovation and user-centred design. He is the founder of D-Cube Designs, a leading design consultancy based in Chennai, India. With a Master's degree in Design from IIT Kanpur, India, which he obtained in 2004, Shah brings a strong academic background and a wealth of practical experience to his work.

As an Industrial Designer, Shah has played a pivotal role in successfully developing and launching over 300 products across various industries over the past decade. His expertise spans the entire product lifecycle, from conducting in-depth user research to designing intuitive and aesthetically pleasing solutions. Shah's keen understanding of customer needs and his ability to translate them into innovative product designs have earned him a reputation for excellence in the industry.

In addition to his contributions to the field of design, Shah has also established himself as a sought-after Business Strategy consultant. Leveraging his customer-centric approach, he has provided valuable insights and guidance to businesses of all sizes, helping them identify market opportunities, develop effective strategies, and drive growth. His expertise in areas such as branding, emotional branding, creativity techniques, leadership, and building competitive advantages has made him a trusted advisor to CEOs, startup founders, and aspiring entrepreneurs.

Shah is an avid blogger and has been sharing his knowledge and insights through his blog for the past eight years. With over four hundred articles covering a wide range of topics, including Branding lessons, Design Thinking, Business Strategy, and Psychology in Business, his blog has become a valuable resource for professionals seeking practical advice and inspiration.

You can connect with me on:
- https://shahmm.medium.com
- https://twitter.com/shahbaba
- https://www.linkedin.com/in/shahmm
- https://www.d-cubedesigns.com

Also by Shah Mohammed

Brand Strategy, Business Strategy and Leadership

The 23 Powerful Laws of Brand Naming: How to Create Brand Names That Stand Out, Connect, and Inspire

In a world where brands are fighting for attention, crafting the perfect name can make all the difference. "The 23 Powerful Laws of Brand Naming" is your ultimate guide to creating brand names that not only stand out from the crowd but also forge deep, lasting connections with your target audience.

Branding expert Shah Mohammed takes you on a captivating journey through the art and science of brand naming, revealing the 23 essential laws that will transform your approach to naming forever. From the fundamentals of memorability and emotional resonance to the intricacies of sound symbolism and linguistic psychology, this book covers every aspect of creating brand names that inspire, engage, and drive success.

Whether you're a startup founder, marketing professional, or branding consultant, "The 23 Powerful Laws of Brand Naming" will equip you with the knowledge you need to create brand names that cut through the noise and leave a lasting impression.

The Heart Market: How to Build an Emotional Brand

In today's crowded marketplace, offering quality products or services is no longer enough. Consumers are seeking deeper connections, emotional resonance, and a sense of belonging that goes beyond mere transactions. Brands that tap into their customers' emotional core will truly thrive in the long run.

Enter "The Heart Market: How to Build an Emotional Brand" by Shah Mohammed - a groundbreaking guide that reveals the secrets to forging powerful emotional bonds between brands and their audiences. This book is a must-read for entrepreneurs, marketers, business leaders, and anyone seeking to create a brand that resonates on a profoundly human level.

The Positioning Playbook: The Winning Strategies for Market Dominance

Unlock the secrets to market supremacy with "The Positioning Playbook: The Winning Strategies for Market Dominance." This comprehensive guide dives into the art and science of strategic positioning, revealing the proven strategies that will set your business apart from the competition and propel you to the top of your industry.

Discover the power of positioning, going beyond superficial branding and slogans, to create a deep and lasting impact on your target audience. Learn how to carve out a distinct space in consumers' minds, forging emotional connections and delivering unique value that resonates with their needs and desires.

Throughout the book, readers are introduced to thirteen effective positioning strategies, each serving as a pathway to achieving market dominance and sustainable success.

Boil The Ocean: The Story of World's Amazing Brands

Embark on a captivating journey through the world of iconic brands with "Boil The Ocean: The Story of World's Amazing Brands." This thought-provoking book offers a collection of insightful case studies that delve into the successes, failures, and transformative moments of some of the most renowned brands in history.

With meticulous research and captivating storytelling, "Boil The Ocean" offers valuable insights, timeless lessons, and inspiring narratives that will engage both business enthusiasts and casual readers. Whether you are an entrepreneur, marketer, designer, brand strategist, startup owner, CEO, brand consultant, or simply intrigued by the stories behind the brands we know and love, this book will leave you inspired, informed, and eager to explore the dynamic world of branding and business.

CEO ASAP: Insider Tips from TOP CEOs for Climbing the Corporate Ladder

Welcome to the ultimate guide for aspiring leaders and young professionals aiming to ascend the corporate ladder swiftly and confidently. "CEO ASAP" is your blueprint for success, curated from the wisdom and experiences of top CEOs who have paved the way to the corner office.

Workplace Whispers: Debunking Myths and Paradoxes

Workplace Whispers: Debunking Myths and Paradoxes" is a captivating exploration of the hidden narratives that shape our professional lives. Across its pages, "Workplace Whispers" examines a diverse array of myths and paradoxes that permeate modern organizational culture. From the allure of Simon Sinek's "Starting with Why" to the pitfalls of the Growth Mindset Myth, each chapter offers a fresh perspective on familiar concepts, prompting readers to question deeply held beliefs and assumptions.

The Secret Strategies of Marketing: How Brands Use Cognitive Biases to Win Your Wallet

In a world bombarded by marketing messages, understanding the psychology that underpins consumer behaviour is the ultimate game-changer. Whether you're a marketer, entrepreneur, business owner, or an inquisitive consumer, this book unravels the mysteries behind why certain brands resonate deeply while others remain forgettable.

Your Guide to Cognitive Biases: This comprehensive guide explores a treasure trove of cognitive biases, from the well-known to the lesser-explored, offering profound insights into their applications and impact. From the allure of familiarity to the power of scarcity, you'll journey through a spectrum of biases that influence every purchase decision.

Innovation's Hidden Walls: Uncovering Limitations of Jobs To Be Done, Design Thinking, and the Diffusion of Innovation Model

In "Innovation's Hidden Walls," we delve deep into the core principles of Jobs To Be Done (JTBD), Design Thinking, and the Diffusion of Innovation Model. While these methodologies have been celebrated for sparking innovation, this book takes a critical look at their limitations. Discover how these walls can restrict your innovation endeavours, and learn how to break through them to truly transform your approach to problem-solving.

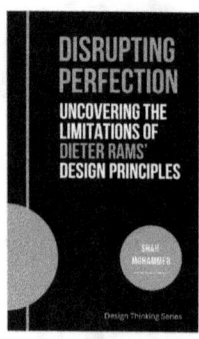

Disrupting Perfection: Uncovering the Limitations of Dieter Rams' Design Principles

"Disrupting Perfection" challenges the conventional wisdom surrounding Dieter Rams' celebrated design principles by delving into their limitations and exploring alternative perspectives on design excellence. This thought-provoking book critiques each of Rams' principles and presents compelling examples that challenge their applicability in contemporary design practice. Through insightful analysis and real-world case studies, readers are invited to reconsider established design norms and embrace a more nuanced understanding of design innovation and user experience.

SUB-BRANDING PLAYBOOK: Winning Strategies for Targeted Growth

In this captivating playbook, you'll discover a treasure trove of sub-branding strategies, each chapter unveiling a different secret weapon to unlock targeted growth. From creating sub-brands for demographic segmentation to psychographic targeting and cultural branding, we leave no stone unturned.

The book provides insights into successful sub-branding initiatives through real-world case studies, offering practical, actionable strategies for leveraging sub-brands to achieve targeted growth. By examining the considerations and criteria for developing sub-brands, readers can understand how sub-brands contribute to brand differentiation, customer targeting, and market expansion.

Elevate your brand's position, attract a loyal customer base, and surpass your competition. The Sub-Branding Playbook is your trusted companion on this exciting adventure, offering guidance, inspiration, and a roadmap to targeted growth.

Breaking Chains: A Manager's Playbook for Becoming a Leader

Embark on a transformative journey from managerial expertise to visionary leadership with "Breaking Chains: A Manager's Playbook for Becoming a Leader." This compelling book redefines leadership, offering invaluable insights and strategies for individuals striving to ascend from managerial roles to impactful leadership positions. Rooted in real-world scenarios and enriched by a wealth of leadership wisdom, this playbook provides a roadmap for professional growth and organizational success.

Unveiling the Managerial Metamorphosis: In the fast-paced landscape of contemporary business, the transition from a manager to a leader is a profound evolution. "Breaking Chains" explores this metamorphosis, unraveling the core shifts that propel individuals from functional mastery to strategic leadership. Drawing inspiration from Michael D. Watkins' HBR article, the playbook delves into transformative factors such as Specialist to Generalist, Analyst to Integrator, Tactician to Strategist, and so on.

www.ingramcontent.com/pod-product-compliance
Lightning Source LLC
Chambersburg PA
CBHW052151220526
45471CB00004B/1622